A STEWARDSHIP SCRAPBOOK

A STEWARDSHIP SCRAPBOOK

WILLIAM R. PHILLIPPE

GENEVA PRESS
LOUISVILLE, KENTUCKY

Scripture quotations from the New Revised Standard Version of the Bible are copyright © 1989 by the Division of Christian Education of the National Council of the Churches of Christ in the U.S.A. and are used by permission. In some instances, the translations have been adapted by the author.

Grateful acknowledgment is made to the following for permission to quote from previously published material:

"There are three kinds of giving . . ." from *Thanks Be to God* by Robert N. Rodenmayer. Copyright © 1960 by Robert N. Rodenmayer, renewed © 1998 by Cathy Bowman. Reprinted by permission of Harper Collins Publishers, Inc.

Alfred A. Knopf, *Trust Me: Short Stories,* by John Updike, 1987.

Office of the General Assembly, Presbyterian Church (U.S.A.), *A Declaration of Faith, 1978.*

Every effort has been made to trace the owner or holder of each copyright. If any rights have been inadvertently infringed upon, the publisher asks that the omission be excused and agrees to make the necessary corrections in subsequent printings.

Book design by Sharon Adams
Cover design and illustration by PAZ Design Group

First edition
Published by Geneva Press
Louisville, Kentucky

This book is printed on acid–free paper that meets the American National Standards Institute Z39.48 standard. ∞

PRINTED IN THE UNITED STATES OF AMERICA

99 00 01 02 03 04 05 06 07 08 — 10 9 8 7 6 5 4 3 2 1

Library of Congress Cataloging-in-Publication Data

Phillippe, William R., 1930-
 A stewardship scrapbook / by William R. Phillippe — 1st ed.
  p. cm.
  ISBN 0-664-50044-7 (alk. paper)
   1. Christian giving. 2. Stewardship, Christian. I. Title.
  BV772.P47 1999
  248'.6—dc21   98–47900

CONTENTS

FOREWORD

Helen Robson Walton, former chair of the Presbyterian Church (U.S.A.) Foundation board and lifetime trustee emeritus, has made a gift that will enable this publication of stewardship materials to become available to the pastors of Presbyterian Church (U.S.A.) congregations. As the Foundation celebrates its two-hundredth anniversary of providing stewardship support for the local church, it is hoped that the use of this publication will increase the support of God's mission and ministry worldwide.

This book is given in appreciation for all the gifts God has first given to us. The Foundation expresses its gratitude for God's faithful servants who have recognized their role as stewards over the past two hundred years. We also thank Bill Phillippe for sharing his creative talents in writing and assembling these materials. Bill has been and continues to be a good friend of the mission of the Presbyterian Church (U.S.A.) and of the ministry of the Presbyterian Church (U.S.A.) Foundation.

Bob Langwig
Stewardship Ministries Consultant
Presbyterian Church (U.S.A.) Foundation

PREFACE

"All the pastor does is talk about money" is a comment I hear too often, and too often the pastor answers, "I don't like to talk about money." From a perspective of four decades of experience, I have learned that most people who think the church talks too much about money are guilty of not giving what they know they should. Many pastors overestimate the sensitivity of their congregations.

I've never minced words about the church's need for money, and I've tried hard not to sentimentalize, symbolize, or soft-pedal how I make my presentations. Overall my results have been successful, and I have gained a lot of respect from members of the congregation who care about the total mission of the church.

Many have asked where I get all the material I use in training, talks, and sermons. So, pressed by Bob Langwig of the Presbyterian Foundation (and others), I've organized my stewardship file.

CLAIMER AND DISCLAIMER:

Like many of you who read this book, I have clipped and shoved sermon bits and pieces into a file folder, in my case for some forty years. Sometimes I have noted the source; some of the time I have forgotten it. The resources have just become part of my mental "hard disk." So, if you see something with the source unacknowledged and you know the source, please tell me. I would like to credit it. Sometimes, however, my own words have been used by another, and when I repeat them, I am told someone else said them. Well fine. That's what the preaching ministry is like. More than once I have been told by a pastor, "Now Bill, when you come to preach—you know that sermon of yours about such and such—well they've already heard that one!" I try to be careful and accurate, but I'm not infallible.

So preachers and lay leaders in stewardship, take heart and have courage. Use this scrapbook as you will—and for heaven's sake, be cheerful about it.

PART ONE

BIBLICAL TEXTS

Chapter 1

Psalm 24

To my mind, the most basic stewardship text is Psalm 24. Most people have memorized the first few verses and can whip them off. You can even get them to repeat it after you:

> The earth is the LORD's, and the fullness thereof;
> the world, and all who dwell therein. (Ps. 24:1)

A corollary statement, not from the Bible, is:

> Stewardship is not "Making the Budget."

But before we go on, a necessary word about nomenclature:

Two words to avoid are "gifts" and "collection." In the first place if "the world, and all who dwell therein" are God's, then we can't give God a gift of what already belongs to God. So let's not announce that "we will bring our gifts to God." That subverts the meaning of the first stewardship text (Psalm 24—remember).

I am equally disturbed when someone announces that we will now take the "collection." A story:

> Once I lived next door to a family with two children and a very large German shepherd dog named Prince. Fortunately I was on good terms with Prince.
>
> One day Prince was on the patio next to my house. I could tell by the smell (and the smoke) that my neighbor was going to grill. Clark, the male child, came around the house with a very large steak and was about to give it to Prince when his dad, close on his heels, grabbed the steak and took it back around the side of the house.

Some time later, Clark appeared again, this time with a plate of bones. He put them down in front of Prince and said, "Prince I intended to give you an offering, but you will have to settle for a collection."

Ah, an offering is, by definition, as paraphrased from several dictionaries:

of'fer.ing, n [AS. *offrung,* a sacrifice.] 1. Act of one who offers; a proffering; specif.: a presenting of something as an act of worship or devotion; sacrifice; oblation.

Now, back to the first text of stewardship: "The earth is the LORD's, and the fullness thereof; the world, and all who dwell therein" (Ps. 24:1). When I was in New York City, I was told of a law firm that was engaged to clear the title of some property in New Orleans. The New York firm, in turn, engaged a New Orleans attorney to get the data from the records. The New Orleans lawyer traced it back as far as 1803, but the New York firm wrote him to say that he had not gone back far enough. In due time they received a letter that said:

Gentlemen:
Please be advised that in the year 1803 the United States of America acquired the territory of Louisiana from the Republic of France by purchase. . . . The Republic of France in turn acquired title from the Spanish Crown by conquest. . . . The Spanish Crown obtained it by virtue of the discoveries of one Christopher Columbus—a Genoese sailor who had been authorized to embark by Isabella, Queen of Spain, who obtained sanction from the Pope, the Vicar of Christ, who is the son and heir of Almighty God, who made Louisiana.

Now that is just another reminder of the truth of the psalmist:

The earth is the LORD's, and the fullness thereof;
the world, and all who dwell therein. (Ps. 24:1)

Jesus also had much to say about the use of money and the person's relationship to the material world. He pointed constantly in his teachings to

the principle of "God's ownership . . . our partnership," or in the tradi-
tional word of our faith family, stewardship!

Many of us recall when present-day "flight attendants" were known as
"stewards," and readers of historical novels discover that when people
went to Europe by ship they were surrounded by the services of a steward, who brought them soup or tea and cakes on deck and ministered to
them in the throes of seasickness below decks. But there is a much wider
concept behind this term "steward" that defines it as any who serve as
manager or trustee for something that is not their own but given to them
to administer for the benefit of others. The foundation for this concept is
laid right in the beginning of the Bible in Genesis 1:1 (KJV):

> In the beginning God created the heaven and the earth. (KJV)

And if that is not enough, Psalm 24, as we have seen, makes it unmistak-
ably clear that the earth belongs to God. In the Genesis story we see that,
as soon as humans are created by God, they are put into the Garden of
Eden "to keep it and to till it." That is, they are put there to manage it. Their
high calling is to manage the earth for God, to be God's trustee. So, from
the beginning of our faith journey, our mothers and fathers in the faith
were appointed as God's managers, agents, trustees in the administration
of the creation.

The clear implication of this is that humans are permitted—even en-
couraged—to manage this vast estate as inventively and creatively as
modern science and technology enable them to do, provided that they
never forget that they are only the managers, that God is the owner and
director whose will it is that the estate be administered for the public good
and not for private gain. Ah, there's the rub! Since we have been given the
God-like power to domesticate and cultivate and, in a sense, to reshape
and re-create God's creation, we easily slip over into the absurd and blas-
phemous notion that we have literally made what we have only remade,
that we have earned possession of the earth by our labors when, in reality, it is only a trust fund to be administered for others.

One passage in the Old Testament that speaks about wealth and riches comes from Genesis 13. It refers to a very early time in our faith history and tells about Abraham and his return from Egypt after he and his family had gone down there during a time of famine in the Promised Land. Listen:

> From Egypt, Abram returned to the Negev with his wife and all he possessed and Lot with him. Abram was a very rich man with livestock, silver, and gold. (Gen. 13:1–2)

Now it may come as a surprise to a lot of stewardship types that Yahweh intended his people to have wealth. It should be clearly noted that God graciously gave this wealth to his people for their enjoyment—but there was a condition:

> But take care you do not forget Yahweh your God. . . . When you have eaten and had all you want, when you have built fine houses to live in, when you have seen your flocks and your herds increase, your silver and gold abound and all your possessions grow great, do not become proud of heart. Do not then forget Yahweh your God who brought you out of the land of Egypt. . . . Beware of saying: "My own strength and the might of my own hand won this power for me." (Deut. 8:11–17)

Throughout holy history, particularly in the Old Testament, there are stern warnings directed against those who strive for wealth through greed, trickery, or treachery and those who act proud about riches and glory in their wealth. The Old Testament warns that wealth and riches may be a sign of God's blessing, but they also may be a cause of God's wrath. Note that the book of Job is a protest, a protest against the commonly held assumption that goodness brings wealth and wickedness brings poverty. So, on balance, the Old Testament presents a very realistic approach to wealth and to riches.

Jesus clearly lived by this teaching and instructed his disciples in the concept of stewardship. But this teaching did not go over well with many in Jesus' day. As is the case now, many were too deeply attached to a contrary manner of living to yield easily to one who attacked it at the root.

In a parable that undoubtedly hastened his death, Jesus compared his opponents to a group of tenant farmers who refused to pay any rent for the vineyard they had leased. They beat up every messenger the owner sent to collect the rent and finally, when the owner sent his son, believing that they would respect him, they killed the son and heir in hopes of claiming his inheritance and of getting clear title to the property for themselves. Refusal of the role of steward, claim of ultimate ownership, is here plainly described as the principal sin that killed our Lord.

So we discover from both Old and New Testament that we are called to be stewards. We are called to a clear recognition that we are not our own, that our time, talents, and possessions are not our own but that "the earth is the Lord's, and the fullness thereof." The earth belongs, under God, to all the earth's inhabitants and not to a privileged few.

A slight digression—but still a part of understanding stewardship: If we continue to live as we are there may not be as much of the earth to steward. David Orr, a professor at Oberlin College in Ohio, says,

> If today is a typical day on planet earth, we will lose 116 square miles of rain forest, or about an acre a second. We will lose another 72 square miles to encroaching deserts, the results of human mismanagement and overpopulation. We will lose 40 to 250 species and no one knows whether the number is 40 or 250. Today the human population will increase by 250,000. And today we will add 2,700 tons of chlorofluorocarbons and 15 million tons of carbon dioxide to the atmosphere. Tonight the earth will be a little hotter, its waters more acidic, and the fabric of life more threadbare. By the year's end the numbers are staggering: The total loss of rain forest will equal an area the size of the state of Washington; expanding deserts will equal an area the size of the state of West Virginia; and the global population will have risen by more than 90,000,000. By

the year 2000 perhaps as much as 20 percent of the life forms extant on the planet in the year 1900 will be extinct. (As reported at the "Pedagogy in a Just and Sustainable World" conference, Claremont School of Theology, November 1997)

Ecumenical Patriarch Bartholomeos, leader of the worldwide Orthodox communion, visited the United States in the fall of 1997, and was even more blunt:

> We are on the verge of the sixth large extinction event in the history of the planet, and for the first time, human actions are the cause. . . . To commit a crime against the natural world is a sin. For humans to cause a species to become extinct, to degrade the integrity of the Earth by causing changes in its climate, stripping its natural forests or destroying its wetlands or contaminating Earth's waters, land, air, and life with poisonous substances: these are sins. (Reported in *Christian Century*, December 3, 1997)

So my first biblical text is Psalm 24. Let me now give you my first nonbiblical text, which comes from Dostoyevsky's *The Brothers Karamazov:*

> Love all God's creation, the whole and every grain of sand in it. Love every leaf, every ray of God's light. Love the animals, love the plants, love everything. If you love everything, you will perceive the divine mystery in things. Once you perceive it, you will begin to comprehend it better every day. And you will come at last to love the whole world with an all-embracing love.

Now, I cannot conclude this chapter without a quote from John Calvin, who constantly referred to the earth as the "theater of God's activity":

> "[L]et us not be ashamed to take pious delight in the works of God open and manifest in this most beautiful theater. . . . (God) created heaven and earth out of nothing. . . . [H]e brought forth living beings and inanimate things of every kind, that in a wonderful series he distinguished an innumerable variety of things, that he en-

dowed each kind with its own nature, assigned functions, appointed places and stations . . . he has conferred the power of propagating, lest by their death the entire species perish; that he has so wonderfully adorned heaven and earth with as unlimited abundance, variety, and beauty of all things as could possibly be, quite like a spacious and splendid house, provided and filled with the most exquisite and at the same time most abundant furnishings. (*Institutes,* Book 1, chap. 14, 20)

So once more—with feeling:

The earth is the LORD's, and the fullness thereof; the world, and all who dwell therein.

Chapter 2

Matthew 6:19–24

Do not store up for yourselves treasures on earth, where moth and rust consume and where thieves break in and steal; but store up for yourselves treasures in heaven, where neither moth nor rust consumes and where thieves do not break in and steal. For where your treasure is, there your heart will be also.

The eye is the lamp of the body. So, if your eye is healthy, your whole body will be full of light; but if your eye is unhealthy, your whole body will be full of darkness. If then the light in you is darkness, how great is the darkness!

*No one can serve two masters; for a slave will either hate the one and love the other, or be devoted to the one and despise the other. You cannot serve God and wealth. —**Matt. 6:19–24***

Treasure on earth—Jesus does not mean that we are to make no provision for our old age or for our children or that we are to avoid accumulation of wealth. This Jesus never condemned. On the contrary, Jesus represented money as a sacred trust and commended the good and faithful servant who diligently improved it. Remember the story of the talents in Matthew 25:14–30? The owner entrusted his slaves with very large amounts of money (a talent represented about fifteen years of wages for a worker!). One got five talents. He traded with them and made five more—total ten. Another got two talents. He traded with them and made two more—total four. A third servant got one talent. He dug a hole, socked the talent away, played it safe, and that money did nothing.

Jesus condemned the third servant for his inaction. What Jesus teaches us is that we must not set our hearts on the "treasures of earth," to accumulate them for their own sake, to make them an end of life, to use them selfishly, forgetting our obligation to others. What he condemns is not riches, but trust in riches. Not money, but the love of money.

Why does Jesus condemn the love of money? Because . . .

1. Earthly treasure is transient; some perishes (moth and rust), some passes out of your hands (thieves, stock market), and in the end you have to leave it all behind. You really can't take it with you.

2. Earthly treasure steals your heart. In the psychology of Jesus' day, the heart was the seat of the emotions, the intellect, and the will. Therefore your treasure could engross the affections, command the thoughts, determine your purpose. To be sure, if your aim is merely to accumulate earthly treasure, you soon discover an anxiety that it will disappear. Your hopes and fears, ambitions and doubts, become concentrated on wealth. It steals your soul!

3. Earthly treasure blinds your vision. Jesus uses a physical fact to illustrate a moral trait. "The eye is the lamp of the body," he says. If it is healthy, if it focuses properly, then your whole body will be full of light. You will have clear and accurate vision. But if it is unhealthy, diseased, blinded, or if it improperly focuses, if it sees double, then you walk uncertainly. You walk in darkness. So if you recognize that living in God's kingdom now is the highest moral value in life, then you have clear vision and can distinguish between good and evil.

However, if your real treasure is your treasures, then feeling, emotions, intellect, and will are all affected. Your moral judgments are distorted, conscience is no longer a safe guide, and you walk in darkness!

4. It is impossible, then, to serve both God and mammon. However, you can serve God with mammon! This reminds me of that wonderful spiritual book written by Søren Kierkegaard more than a hundred years ago. The title tells the story: *Purity of Heart Is to Will One Thing*. This thought leads me to my second "nonbiblical" text, one from Frederick Buechner's book *Wishful Thinking:*

> The trouble with being rich is that since you can solve with your
> checkbook virtually all the practical problems that bedevil ordinary

people, you are left in your leisure with nothing but the great human problems to contend with: how to be happy, how to love and be loved, how to find meaning and purpose in your life.

In desperation the rich are continually tempted to believe that they can solve these problems too with their checkbooks, which is presumably what led Jesus to remark one day that for a rich man to get to Heaven is about as easy as for a Cadillac to go through a revolving door. (*Wishful Thinking,* New York: Harper & Row, 1973, p. 81)

Now, to be honest, many, if not most, of us are pretty big camels. Matthew Fox commented, "We have become compulsive consumers, walking garbage cans, espousing the philosophy, 'I buy; therefore, I am.'" Let's look seriously at how much we buy and what we buy. In 1995, Sylvia and John Ronsvalle reported that religious people in the United States spend about $2 billion on mission overseas, but as a population we spend . . .

- $500 million more than that on chewing gum
- more than $4 billion on movies
- $8 billion on adventure travel
- $12 billion on candy
- $20 billion on cosmetics
- $49 billion on soft drinks

(From a presentation by John and Sylvia Ronsvalle of Empty Tomb, at the 1995 Presbyterian Church [U.S.A.] Research Conference on Giving)

We could go on and list our own attachments—computer upgrades, camcorders, sports utility vehicles. The Ronsvalles point out that from 1968 to 1991 American gross family income (adjusted for all those things economists like to do) grew 44 percent while giving to the church during that period grew by only 18 percent, which means Americans were making more and giving less of it to the church. It is clear that we have more disposable income today and we are disposing of it, but we are not "disposing" of it by giving it to the church. As some wag said, "The problem with most of us is that our net income does not keep up with our gross habits!"

Let me give you a few more statistics from the Ronsvalles. The average Protestant family:

> in 1916 gave 2.9%
> of income
> in 1933, the depth of the Great Depression, gave 3.3%
> of income
> in 1955, the beginning of affluence, gave 3.2%
> of income
> in 1993, when Americans were 200% richer than in the Great
> Depression, gave 2.5%
> of income

John Calvin had a lot to say about this. One Reformation Sunday I preached about Calvin's insistence that the gospel had to be put in new wine skins. As an illustration, I described the "Sumptuary Laws" Calvin got passed in Geneva. These laws tried to prohibit ostentatious living by regulating such matters as how much lace could be on a gown and how many courses could be served at a meal. It was all very practical—and biblical!

There is a sense in which you and I are owned by whatever we cannot, or will not, give away, a sense in which who we are is defined very precisely by what we can or cannot give away. This is truly a spiritual issue—an issue that should concern all of us who are called to be the extended family of God. Frankly, it is not just startling but depressing and disheartening to hear the Ronsvalles report that "churchgoers have changed from being stewards to being consumers." I also found a challenge in their statement that "ministers must 'desacralize' money, for in the words of Jacques Ellul, 'Money is the last sacred subject in Western culture.'"

All the time people tell me, "Money talks." All right . . . agreed. Now, it's time we began to talk back to it.

A Prayer of Confession:

O God, you hold creation close to your heart. But we have kept the best offerings and ripest fruits for ourselves, while you have waited and creation has wasted away. We have frantically hoarded while our world has been depleted. We have leisurely washed our hands while our world has been defiled. We have hastened to endless feasts while our world has been denied. O God, save us from one another, and save your world from our sin.

Chapter 3

First Timothy 6:6–10

Of course, there is great gain in godliness combined with contentment; for we brought nothing into the world, so that we can take nothing out of it; but if we have food and clothing, we will be content with these. But those who want to be rich fall into temptation and are trapped by many senseless and harmful desires that plunge people into ruin and destruction. For the love of money is a root of all kinds of evil, and in their eagerness to be rich some have wandered away from the faith and pierced themselves with many pains. —1 Tim. 6:6–10

Money is all-pervasive in modern life. It gets mixed up with everything. It is, however, the most indispensable of all the tools we have; we could not exist for a day without using it or having others use it for us. Last spring, my wife and I were in Savannah, staying at a small historic hotel on one of the squares. We had walked to dinner at a nearby restaurant and were enjoying the walk back through the soft night, when, as we were crossing the street by the hotel with nothing in sight and not a sound in the air but the crickets, a car came out of nowhere. An arm reached out of the passenger side of the car and took Kay's purse from her shoulder. The car then sped into the night. We were just beginning a two-week vacation, and we had to cancel all the credit cards and the ATM card. I know you can't exist without money in our world! Ours is a money culture and for that very reason, just because money is power and does talk, it is easy to make it the one-and-only yardstick of everything. "Money is one of our deepest passions," says Robert Wuthnow, professor of sociology at Princeton University:

Loved, sought after, sometimes ridiculed and despised, it has always been considered fundamental to the lives of individuals and of societies. Following customs nearly three millennia old, printed currencies carry the faces of public figures who symbolize the commonweal. The great age of exploration that led to the founding of our new nation was prompted in no small measure by the belief that bullion and power went hand in hand. (*Poor Richard's Principle: Recovering the American Dream through the Moral Dimension of Work, Business, and Money,* Princeton, N.J.: Princeton University Press, 1996, p. 138)

Wuthnow goes on to point out in his survey that Americans, in spite of our passion and love for money, still practice an ancient taboo against speaking about money in public. There seems to be no problem anymore in rehearsing our sex life in public, but we still express a reverence, an awe, about our money. Again from *Poor Richard's Principle:*

> [A]ttitudes toward money become a matter of personal choice, just as one's religious opinions do. The choice itself is likely to be warranted as an arbitrary personal proclivity, such as taste, because none of the competing public warrants is grounded in a firm sense of absolute reality. . . . One learns not to judge the way people spend their money, treating their choices as functions of lifestyle, upbringing, or disposable income itself. The taboo against money-talk reflects these norms of civility. (p. 152)

However, money is the subject that Jesus talked about most; it is mentioned more than 150 times in the New Testament. Jesus was very blunt about it, did not mince his words, and did not use circumlocution. I think it is high time that we desacralize money, that we talk about it—talk about it openly and talk about it openly in the church! In an earlier book, Wuthnow discusses feelings of citizens in this country toward both money and their work. He claims that three out of four people that he talked to would like the church to encourage people to be less materialistic, but he maintains that this will probably not happen because of the taboo against talking openly about money:

When asked how often in the past year they had discussed various aspects of their personal finances with people outside their immediate family, 82% said they had never or hardly ever discussed their income, 89% said they had not discussed their family budget, 76% said this about their major purchases, 75% said they had not discussed worries they might have had about money, and 92% said the same about their giving to charities. (*God and Mammon in America*, New York: Free Press, 1994, p. 139)

So I understand why pastors are reluctant to talk to people about money, but pastors must do so. If they, or others in the church, do not, who will?

Some people think the Bible says that money is the root of all evil, but that is not what it says. The Bible does not teach that money is evil. In itself it is neither good nor bad; it all depends on what is done with it, the way in which it is employed, the way we think of it. Notice how William Barclay translates 1 Timothy 6:6–10:

Those who wish to be rich fall into temptation and a snare, and into many senseless and harmful desires for the forbidden things, desires which swamp men in a sea of ruin and total loss in time and in eternity. For the love of money is a root from which all evils spring; and some, in their reaching out after it, have been sadly led astray, and have transfixed themselves with many pains.

And Clarence Jordan, in *The Cotton Patch Version* of Paul's epistles, puts it:

When people make money their goal, they fall head over heels into confusion and into a bear trap and into all kinds of senseless and harmful cravings which shove them down into ruin and destruction. For the root of everything wicked is money-addiction. And some folks, in forming the habit, have ceased to be Christians and have hanged themselves with a peck of troubles.

Robert McCracken once said, "Money can be a beautiful thing, it is we who make it grimy. We send it to places where it has no business to go and tarnish it with unhallowed transactions."

So the Bible condemns not money but the love of it—the greedy, grasping, covetous instinct that makes acquisition the goal of life and sees in wealth an end in itself.

> Not long ago, there appeared in the newspapers a story of a landing problem with a commercial airliner. The paper reported that when the landing gear of the plane collapsed upon landing and the flight crew ordered an evacuation down the emergency slides, almost half the passengers reacted by grabbing their carry-on luggage. One man grabbed two bags, another struggled with a large bag. A woman blocked the aisle struggling to get a garment bag out of an overhead bin. What have we come to when we would jeopardize our own life as well as the life of others by our inordinate attachment to baggage!

Now my "nonbiblical" illustration:

> Once upon a time, two flies were walking by a piece of flypaper, called, appropriately, "Tanglefoot."
> The young fly said to the older one, "What do you think of this stuff called Tanglefoot?"
> "I'm opposed to it," the older said.
> "Why? What's the matter, is it poisonous?"
> "Not a bit."
> "Is it bitter?"
> "No, it's rather sweet."
> "Then what are your objections?"
> About that time a friend of theirs settled down right in the middle of the flypaper. "My flypaper," he said proudly.
> But the flypaper said, "My fly."
> And the older fly said, "Ah, he is possessed by his possession."

So, in the end, understanding stewardship is a spiritual matter. Many of our people have lost the all-encompassing vision that everything belongs to God. We have been seduced into thinking that what we have is ours, and that we need more.

President Jimmy Carter, in the midst of the "energy crisis" of the 1970s, gave a remarkable address to the nation on July 18, 1979. In part he said,

> In a nation that was proud of hard work, strong families, close-knit communities and faith in God, too many of us now worship self-indulgence and consumption. Human identity is no longer defined by what one does but by what one owns . . . [but] owning things and consuming things does not satisfy our longing for meaning. We have learned that piling up material goods cannot fill the emptiness of lives which have no confidence or purpose. (As reported in *The Simple Life: Plain Living and High Thinking in American Culture,* by David E. Shi, New York: Oxford University Press, 1985, p. 271)

Stewardship is not making the budget—it is a way of life for all of life.

SOME ADDITIONAL STEWARDSHIP TEXTS

ON TITHING:

Leviticus 27:30–32
Numbers 18:20–32
Deuteronomy 14:22–29; 26:12–15

ON GOD'S OWNERSHIP OF ALL THINGS:

Leviticus 25:23

PARABLES OF JESUS FROM THE GOSPEL OF LUKE:

Luke 7:41–43, two forgiven debtors
Luke 10:29–37, the good Samaritan
Luke 12:13–21, the rich fool
Luke 12:42–48, the faithful and wise steward

Luke 13:6–9, the fruitless fig tree
Luke 16:1–9, the unjust steward
Luke 16:19–31, the rich man and Lazarus

ON A LIFE OF SIMPLICITY, SOBRIETY, AND TEMPERATENESS:

Matthew 6:12–21, 25–33
Luke 18:18–25
Titus 2:11–14

And finally this delightful passage from Paul where his true humanity shines through. He is dealing with the collection for the congregation at Jerusalem. But now it becomes clear that Paul has been encouraging the Corinthians to generosity by quoting the example of the Macedonians— and that he has been encouraging the Macedonians to generosity by quoting the example of the Corinthians! Now he is just a little afraid that the Corinthians may let him down!

> Now I know of course that it is really quite superfluous for me to be writing to you about this matter of giving to fellow Christians, for I know how willing you are. Indeed I have told the Macedonians with some pride that "Achaia was ready to undertake this service twelve months ago." Your enthusiasm has consequently been a stimulus to many of them. I am, however, sending the brothers just to make sure that our pride in you is not unjustified. For, between ourselves, it would never do if some of the Macedonians were to accompany me on my visit to you and find you unprepared for this act of generosity! We (not to speak of you) should be horribly ashamed, just because we had been so proud and confident of you. This is my reason, then, for urging the brothers to visit you before I come myself, so that they can get your promised gift ready in good time. But, having let you into my confidence, I should like it to be a spontaneous gift, and not money squeezed out of you by what I have said. All I shall say is that poor sowing means a poor harvest, and generous sowing means a generous harvest.

Let everyone give as his heart tells him, neither grudgingly nor under compulsion, for God loves the one who gives cheerfully. After all, God can give you everything that you need, so that you may always have sufficient both for yourselves and for giving away to other people.

He who gives the seed to the sower and turns that seed into bread to eat will give you the seed of generosity to sow and, for harvest, the satisfying bread of good deeds done. The more you are enriched by God, the more scope will there be for generous giving, and your gifts, administered through us, will mean that many will thank God. For your giving does not end in meeting the wants of your fellow Christians. It also results in an overflowing tide of thanksgiving to God and proves the reality of your faith. (2 Cor. 9:1–9; J. B. Phillips translation)

AND MY FAVORITE FOR UNDERSTANDING THE RELATIONSHIP OF THOSE OF US WHO "HAVE" WITH THOSE WHO "HAVE NOT":

Deuteronomy 24:19–22

PART TWO

SERMONS

Chapter 4

If I Were a Rich Man

Someone in the crowd said to him, "Teacher, tell my brother to divide the family inheritance with me." But he said to him, "Friend, who set me to be a judge or arbitrator over you?" And he said to them, "Take care! Be on your guard against all kinds of greed; for one's life does not consist in the abundance of possessions." Then he told them a parable: "The land of a rich man produced abundantly. And he thought to himself, 'What should I do, for I have no place to store my crops?' Then he said, 'I will do this: I will pull down my barns and build larger ones, and there I will store all my grain and my goods. And I will say to my soul, 'Soul, you have ample goods laid up for many years; relax, eat, drink, be merry.' But God said to him, 'You fool! This very night your life is being demanded of you. And the things you have prepared, whose will they be?' So it is with those who store up treasures for themselves but are not rich toward God." —Luke 12:13–21

Scripture says a great deal about riches—
    and about wealth.
In the Old Testament both of these terms are used to designate
    abundance of property
    in land and buildings and livestock.
These were the basic economic commodities of an agricultural society and
economy all over the ancient world.
But the unique Old Testament attitude toward wealth
    is a religious understanding of it.

Since Yahweh is creator and sovereign over all creation,
　　then all things belong to Yahweh.
You can find this clearly illustrated in the Psalms:

> The earth is the LORD's, and the fullness thereof;
> 　　the world, and all who dwell therein. (Ps. 24:1)

Such an affirmation was understood by the people of Israel
　　in a very pragmatic way.
They kept saying it was Yahweh
　　who had given his people the land of Canaan
　　　　after the exodus from Egypt—
and as Yahweh graciously gave Israel her inheritance,
　　the Promised Land,
　　　　so he blesses individuals with wealth.
The foremost example in the Old Testament
　　is that of Abraham.
Take his statement from the thirteenth chapter of Genesis:

> From Egypt Abram returned to the Negev with his wife and all he
> possessed and Lot with him. Abram was a very rich man, with live-
> stock, silver and gold. (vv. 1–2, JB)

Ah, it may come as a surprise to some that
　　Yahweh intended his people to have wealth!
It should be clearly noted that God graciously
　　gave the wealth of the earth to his people for their enjoyment,
but they in turn are required never to forget who gave them this wealth.

In Deuteronomy we have this poignant statement:

> Take care you do not forget Yahweh your God. . . . When you have
> eaten and had all you want, when you have built fine houses to live
> in, when you have seen your flocks and herds increase, your silver
> and gold abound and all your possessions grow great, do not be-

come proud of heart. Do not then forget Yahweh your God who
brought you out of the land of Egypt, out of the house of slavery:
who guided you through this vast and dreadful wilderness, a land
of fiery serpents, scorpions, thirst: who in this waterless place
brought you water from the hardest rock; who in this wilderness fed
you with manna. . . . Beware of saying in your heart, "My own
strength and the might of my own hand won this power for me."
Remember Yahweh your God: it was he who gave you this strength
and won you this power. Be sure that if you forget Yahweh your
God, if you follow other gods, if you serve them and bow down before them—I warn you this day—you will most certainly perish.
(Deut. 8:11–19)

Throughout Israel's history, stern warnings are directed against
   those who strive for wealth
    through greed, and trickery, and treachery,
   and those who act proud and glory in their wealth.

The Old Testament warns that wealth and riches
   may be a sign of God's blessing but they also
   may be the cause of God's wrath.
Israel's, or an individual's, faithfulness or unfaithfulness
   is central in the determining of which it shall be.

As a matter of fact, the book of Job strongly protests against the general
view
   that goodness brings wealth
    and wickedness brings poverty.

And in a number of psalms the word "rich" is synonymous with "wicked"
   and "poor" synonymous with "righteousness" and "godly."

So, on balance, in the Old Testament

there is a very realistic approach to riches and wealth,
    namely, that possessions should be enjoyed and shared,
    but that the people must always remember
        that the source of all is God.
When we move to the New Testament,
    Jesus' teachings, while consistent with the Old Testament,
        lay added emphasis on the dangers of riches and wealth.
At one point Jesus looked around and said to the disciples,
    "How hard it is for those who have riches to enter the Kingdom of God"
    (Matt. 19:23).
And the disciples were astounded by those words.

But Jesus insisted:

    My children, it is easier for a camel
    to pass through the eye of a needle,
    than for a rich man to enter the kingdom of God. (Matt. 19:24)

There is a delightful story of a feud in Scotland between two clans,
    the Campbells and the McGregors.
One preacher from the McGregor side leaned over the pulpit one time and
said,
    "Scripture says it: It's easer for a rich man
    to pass through the eye of a needle
    than for a Campbell to enter the kingdom of God."

But at any rate, the story clearly illustrates Jesus' point of view that he is
    frankly pessimistic about the ability of persons who possess wealth
    to escape being beholden to it.
For the problem is not wealth, per se,
    but what wealth can do to us
        when it is our possessions that possess us
            instead of God who possesses us.

It is in that context that Jesus tells the parable about the rich man.
Jesus opens the parable with a terse statement:

> Take care! Be on your guard against all kind of greed; for one's life
> does not consist in the abundance of possessions. (Luke 12:15)

Just because a person has abundance,
    that doesn't mean that his life will be whole.
As a matter of fact,
    wealth is no guarantee of his continuance of life.

The story that Jesus tells, then,
    is the story of a coward, a person who is trying to make his life secure.
He fills his barns and builds new barns,
    fills them, and then says to himself,

> "Self, you've got enough stuff
>   stashed away to do you for a long time.
>   Recline, dine,
>   wine, and shine!"
> But God said to him,
>   "You nitwit—
>   at this very moment your goods are putting the screw on
>   your soul."

In other words, he finds the security that he is out for,
    but Jesus calls him a fool,
        for he loses the very meaning of life!

William Barclay, Scottish biblical scholar,
    pointed out that at least two things stand out about the man:
First of all,
    he never saw beyond himself.
There is no parable of Jesus that is as full as this one is of the words
    "I" and "me" . . . "my" and "mine."

A schoolboy was once asked what parts of speech
    "my" and "mine" are, and he said,
        "Aggressive pronouns."
Well the rich fool was
    aggressively self-centered,
        a person completely stuck on himself,
            whose response to every question was,
        How will this affect me
            and my place in the world,
                my possessions, my prestige?
This rich man had no ego problem, he was all id.
The man in the story had enough of the world's goods,
    more than enough,
        and the one thing that never entered his head
            was to give anything away.
His whole attitude was the reverse of the teaching of Jesus.
Instead of finding his happiness in giving,
    instead of understanding the Old Testament teaching
        that all he had was really a gift from God
            to be shared with others
                and to be enjoyed in this land,
    he tried to conserve it all
        by keeping it locked away in his barns.

The Romans had a proverb that went:
    "Money is like seawater;
    the more you drink, the thirstier you become."

As long as a person's attitude is that of the rich fool,
    his desire will always be to get more,
        and that's really the reverse of the way of life taught by Jesus.

But, if this rich man never saw beyond himself,
    this man, in the second place, never saw beyond this world.
All his plans were made on the basis of
    life in this world.

Let me tell you a story of a conversation between such a person and another who knew life in its fullness.

    The one asked the other,
        "What are you going to do with your life?"
    The other replied,
        "I'll learn my trade well."
    "And then?"
        "I'll set myself up in business."
    "And then?"
        "I'll make my fortune."
    "And then?"
        "I suppose I shall grow old and retire and live on my
        money."
    "And then?"
        "Well, I suppose someday I will die."
    Then came the last stabbing question:
    "And then . . . ?"

The person who never remembers that there is
    another world
    is destined someday for the grimmest of grim shocks.
For Yahweh will ask us,

        What have you done with your life—
            your time
            your talent
            your skills
            your treasure?

So Jesus ends his story about the rich man by saying,

> This very night you must surrender your life;
> your soul is required of you! (Luke 12:20)

It is in contrast to this that Jesus
   positively taught his disciples saying,

> Get yourselves purses that do not wear out.
> Get yourselves treasure that will not fail you,
>   in heaven,
> where no thief can reach it, no moth destroy it,
> for where your treasure is,
>   there will your heart be also. (Luke 12:33–34)

But the question still comes:
   Am I a rich person?
      I don't have much . . .
None of us wants to admit to being a "rich man."

One of the real problems we must face
   is the gap between
      opulence and poverty,
   for that is really what we are dealing with here.
The picture in the round is that
   less than 30 percent of the world's population
      controls and consumes more than 70 percent of the world's resources,
   and 6 percent of that 30 percent—the United States—
      holds a disproportionate share of that maldistribution.
Further, the gap between the rich and the poor of our globe
   is growing wider year by year.

If I were a rich man?
   In the eyes of the world, every one of us is!
Some time ago, a group of us
   worked on a project to help Americans understand that truth.

We put together a picture
   of what genuine poverty would look like
      if it struck one of our homes.

Take a look at how the majority of our world lives—
   walk into this house with me.
The first thing that we do is to strip it of its furniture:
   everything goes—
   beds and chairs,
   tables and TV sets, lamps.
We will leave the family with a few old blankets,
   a kitchen table, a wooden chair.
Along with all the chests go all the clothes.
Each member of the family may keep as a wardrobe
   the oldest suit or dress,
      a shirt or blouse.
We'll permit a pair of shoes for the head of the family
   but none for the wife or children.
Move to the kitchen.
   The appliances all go.
Then turn to the cupboards.
   The box of matches may stay—
      a small bag of flour,
      some sugar, some salt;
   a few moldy potatoes already in the garbage
      have to be hastily rescued
      for they will provide much of tonight's meal.
We'll leave a handful of onions,
   a dish of dried beans.
All the rest we take away—
   the meat, the fresh vegetables, the canned foods,
   the crackers, the candy.

Now we've stripped the house,
    but the bathroom must be dismantled—
        the running water shut off,
        the electric wires taken out.
Next we take away the house.
    The family can move into the garage.
Communications go next—
    no newspaper, magazines, or books . . .
        not that they will be missed,
        since we also must take away the family literacy.
Instead, we will allow one radio for the whole neighborhood.
Now government services must go.
    No more postman, no more fireman.
There is a school, but it is three miles away
    and consists of two classrooms.
There are, of course, no hospitals or doctors nearby—
    the nearest clinic is ten miles away
    and is tended by a midwife.
And finally, money.
    We'll allow our family a cash hoard of $5.00.

If I were a rich man?
    But I am!
It really depends on my perspective.
I am very rich,
    for piled high on my doorstep
        lie the greatest of riches,
            and they are there for my taking.
Towering up in the air so high that my neighbors stand around
    thunderstruck at the sight saying,
        "Who in the world would give you all of that?
        How can you have so much?"

Have you ever counted your riches . . .
  your wealth?

In 1 Corinthians, Paul says:

> For all things are yours, everything belongs to you,
> Paul, Apollos, Peter, the world. Life and death, the
> present and the future, all of this belongs to you.
> For you belong to Christ and Christ to God. (1 Cor. 3:21–23)

It is all there for your taking.
Although you may never hear it,
  there is a litany of
  land and sea and air
    forever ringing in your ears.
It's wonderful to walk the earth
  and hear the beat of it,
    for the world is yours.
Its circumference, all twenty-five thousand miles of it, is yours.
All of its revolving sun and moon and stars are yours.
All of its law of growth and of gravity,
  all of its laws of light and sound,
  all of its laws of high tide and low tide, are yours.
All of its chemistry, physics, and geology are yours.
All of its atmosphere, with fourteen pounds of air
  pressing down on every square inch of your body to keep you safe, is
    yours.
All of its oceans and seven seas and lakes and rivers are yours.
All of its mountains and valleys and templed hills are yours.
All of its orchards and forests and vineyards are yours.
But you have a stewardship in this
  lending from the Lord.
Not to squander trees,

or let the fields turn into dust bowls
   or let acid rain poison the lakes.
All of its silver and gold,
   all of its copper and uranium are yours.
But you have a stewardship in this
   lending from the hand of God.
Not to use the earth's resources
   to destroy earth's children.

All things are yours, all of life.
All this wonderful, throbbing, beating, quenchable force
   inside of you is yours
   for three score years and ten and more.
All of its births, its childhood, its adolescence,
   its maturity and senility are yours.
All of its nearly six billion people and
   kindred and tribes are yours.
All of its languages, tongues, and dialects.
All of its cannibals and headhunters,
   dictators, assassins, terrorists, and thieves are yours.
All of its emperors and presidents,
   its governments and bureaucrats.
All of its professors, teachers, students, and illiterates.
All of its doctors, nurses,
   diseases, hungers, and thirsts are yours.
All of its invalids,
   deaf, dumb, blind, and lame are yours.
All of its preachers
   and its 1.9 billion Christians are yours.
All of its blood, sweat, and tears.
All of its joy and bliss and creativity are yours.

All things are yours, death.
All of its wonder, dread, beauty, and release from pain are yours.

All of its safe lying down to sleep at night
    and safe waking up in the morning are yours.
All of its angels and archangels
    and the great cloud of witnesses that surround you.
All the understanding of things never understood,
All the wonder, the love, the praise, the adoration are yours.
All the peace that passes understanding is yours.

All things are yours, things present.
All the status quo is yours.
All the tension between first and second and third worlds is yours.
All the Middle East situation is yours.
All the tension in Bosnia, Ireland, and Central Africa is yours.
All the race prejudice is yours.
All the poverty, slums, hard-core unemployable are yours.
All the music, art, poetry, and beauty are yours.
All the churches, hospitals, charities,
    libraries, and public parks are yours.
All the United Nations,
    the Church World Service,
        and Amnesty International are yours.

All things are yours, things to come.
All peace on earth and good will
    among all human beings are yours.
All international Christianity is yours,
    the World Council of Churches and
    the World Alliance of Reformed Churches.
All life and liberty
    and the pursuit of happiness are yours.
All quietness and confidence forever are yours.

All things are yours,
    for you are Christ's,
        and Christ is God's.

Ah, yes,
  if I were a rich man . . .
    But I am!
What are you going to do about it?
  What will I do about it?

Chapter 5

The Miracle of Broken Bread

*The apostles gathered around Jesus, and told him all that they had done and taught. He said to them, "Come away to a deserted place all by yourselves and rest a while." For many were coming and going, and they had no leisure even to eat. And they went away in the boat to a deserted place by themselves. Now many saw them going and recognized them, and they hurried there on foot from all the towns and arrived ahead of them. As he went ashore, he saw a great crowd; and he had compassion for them, because they were like sheep without a shepherd; and he began to teach them many things. When it grew late, his disciples came to him and said, "This is a deserted place, and the hour is now very late; send them away so that they may go into the surrounding country and villages and buy something for themselves to eat." But he answered them, "You give them something to eat." They said to him, "Are we to go and buy two hundred denarii worth of bread, and give it to them to eat?" And he said to them, "How many loaves have you? Go and see." When they had found out, they said, "Five, and two fish." Then he ordered them to get all the people to sit down in groups on the green grass. So they sat down in groups of hundreds and of fifties. Taking the five loaves and the two fish, he looked up to heaven, and blessed and broke the loaves, and gave them to his disciples to set before the people; and he divided the two fish among them all. And all ate and were filled; and they took up twelve baskets full of broken pieces and of the fish. Those who had eaten the loaves numbered five thousand men. —**Mark 6:30–44**

Jesus taught his disciples to pray, saying,
   "Give us this day
      our daily bread . . . "

And before each meal,
    our mothers and fathers in the faith
        in ancient times,
            and still today pray,

                Blessed art Thou,
                O Lord our God,
                King of the world,
                who bringest forth bread from the earth.

Bread is mentioned
    250 times in the Old Testament
        and
    77 times in the New Testament.

This sermon is about bread.
    And I want to comment specifically about the text from Mark
    and then tell you three stories about bread.
As Jesus' ministry progressed,
    he was no longer content to depend on
        his own efforts to evangelize the villages of Galilee.
So he called the Twelve together
    and began to send them out two by two.
When they returned from their preaching mission,
    they told Jesus what they had done and taught.
Ever sensitive to the physical needs of those about him,
    Jesus suggested that they go with him
        to find a quiet place where they could find some rest.
But it was not to be found.
Streams of visitors,
    drawn by the growing fame of Jesus' works,
        kept them ever in movement and even broke in on their meals.
According to the literal rendering of the Greek,

they had no "opportunity for leisure or anything."
Jesus' plan to be alone with the Twelve,
    in this instance, was frustrated by the people who recognized his
    intentions.
For while Jesus and his disciples went across
    the lake in a boat,
        they went around the northern end by foot,
    and when Jesus and the disciples landed,
        they found the usual throng of eager people waiting for them.
Though Jesus' expectation of quiet was defeated,
    he did not give way to a sense of disappointment.
Instead, his compassion was stirred by the scene,
    the eager interest of the crowd.
Mark puts it,

>   He had compassion for them,
>   because they were like sheep without a shepherd. (6:34)

So Jesus gave up this time of rest
    and began to teach them.
When the afternoon was about over,
    the disciples came to him to tell him
        it was about time to think of food.
Dismiss the crowd, they said,
    so that they could go into the farms and villages about
        and buy something to eat for themselves.
But Jesus turned to them and said,
    "You give them something to eat."
The disciples were startled by such a suggestion.
    "Shall we go and buy 200 denarii worth of bread?"
        Obviously they thought the suggestion absurd.
But Jesus was insistent:
    "How many loaves have you? Go and see."

They came back and reported,
    "Five, and two fish."
Jesus then directed them to sit the crowd
    by groups on the fresh grass of the hillside.
And when they had,
    Jesus took the five loaves and the two fish,
        looked up, blessed them,
        and broke the loaves in pieces and gave them to the disciples to pass
        to the people.
And they all ate and had enough.
The disciples gathered up twelve baskets of leftovers!
To understand what actually happened here, I think we need to go to another text in Mark,
    one that tells of an event a bit later in Jesus' ministry.
In both Matthew and Mark,
    we have the story of the disciples again going across the lake in a boat.
They were hungry—
    and distressed about it—
        because they had only one loaf of bread along.
But if Jesus had actually turned
    one loaf into many
        by magic or by miracle
    for the feeding of the five thousand,
        and later for the four thousand
    the question comes to mind,
        Why should the disciples be distressed?
    Jesus could do it again!
Jesus hears them muttering and gives them a rebuke:
    "There was plenty of bread the other day in that big crowd," he said.
        "The problem was a spiritual problem—
            a problem of attitude."
There is plenty of bread in the world for everybody;
    the problem is to arrange for everybody who needs it to have their share.

I believe what happened a few days before was that
    Jesus aimed at and achieved
        a change of attitude.
He turned that mixed crowd,
    composed of many individuals,
        each with his own self-regarding interests and impulses,
            into a single community
                for the purpose of sharing in common,
                    what was to begin with,
                        the property of a few.
So those who were strangers,
    under the spell of Jesus' message of
        love and concern and caring,
    were brought to feel for
        and be sensitive to
            the needs of each other,
                and they became a single family of God.
Their attitude was altered.
The gift was multiplied,
    for they realized that they were one.
What a magnificent miracle!
The truth is that this same miracle occurs each and every Sunday,
    right here in this sanctuary,
        and in all others.

God has put us together here in this extended family
    to become a demonstration
        of what God intends for all of humanity.
We are here to discover
    the new humanity—the new creation—
    to show a new beginning for human life in the world where
        sin is forgiven,
        reconciliation is accomplished,

where the dividing walls of hostility are torn down.
We are expected to live and to proclaim to others
    that a new age has dawned—
That God who creates life
    frees those in bondage,
    forgives sin,
    reconciles brokenness,
    makes all things new.
We are expected to live as disciples
    as followers of this new way of life—
    to participate in God's activity in the world by healing and reconciling
    and binding up wounds,
    ministering to the needs of the poor, the sick, the lonely and the
    powerless,
    engaging in the struggle to free people from sin, fear, oppression, hunger,
    and injustice,
    giving of ourselves and our money to the service of others.
We are literally sharing with Christ
    in the establishing of his just, peaceable,
    and loving rule in the world.[1]

What a calling!
What a miracle!

But there is still a greater miracle that happens each Sunday
    in this place.
Jesus has given us a commission
    as present-day disciples to
        "Go into all the world," and preach . . . teach . . . heal.

---

[1]Paraphrase of chapter 3 of *The Form of Government* of the Presbyterian Church (U.S.A.).

For a variety of reasons we all cannot go physically; there are
　　family responsibilities,
　　jobs that must be done here and now,
　　health reasons.
But he requires each of us to go.
Well, you do go . . .
　　You go each Sunday
　　　　when the offering plates are passed
　　　　and you put money in the plates.
You are then instantly in Nepal, in the high mountains . . .
　　in the skilled hands of Dr. Richard and Susanne Harding,
　　　　treating more than 100,000 people in clinics there.
　　Thailand . . .
　　　　teaching, through Scott Satterfield and Mitchel Young.
　　Guatemala City . . .
　　　　working to train ministers through Dennis and Maribel Smith.
　　Cameroon . . .
　　　　teaching, through Paul and Eleanor Frelick.

Instantly, you are there,
　　because you put money in that plate,
　　money that is congealed sweat and toil.
And the church officers transmit and transmute it
　　back into sweat and toil in the lives of
　　more than 1,000 workers overseas,
　　469 full-time missionaries in 65 countries,
　　international subsistence workers,
　　volunteers in mission,
　　bi-national servants,
　　overseas associates.

Do you know that it costs approximately
　　$80,000 to sustain each such person,
　　$95,000 for a couple in the mission fields?

The denomination multiplied those loaves and fishes,
    multiplied that money you put into the plate!
And this made you a part of
    more than 500 overseas schools and hospitals,
    49 nursing schools,
    158 dispensaries and clinics,
    9 seminaries with more than 2,000 candidates for ministry.
Because you put that money in the plate,
    more than 2 million people received medical aid,
        who, without your help, would not have received it.

You were there overseas . . .
    in evangelists,
    urban workers,
    agricultural specialists,
    media people, translators,
    physicians, and nurses.
What a miracle—
    because you put money in the plate!

In this land you helped support
    more than 3,000 people in strategic ministries,
        like 1,000 pastors in small churches
        that were designated strategic in mission,
        but who could not fund a full-time pastor on their own.
    From Appalachia to the Western deserts,
        small communities had full-time pastors
            because you put money in the plate.

You enabled . . .
    231 health ministries,
    2,172 candidates to learn ministry,
    8 institutions to give specialized education to

native Americans,
Hispanic Americans,
black Americans.
And 1,428 refugees from fourteen countries were settled.
Because you put money in the plate,
   49 new congregations were organized last year,
      14,729 adults were baptized,
         and more than 50,000 children were baptized.
More than 180,000 persons said, knowing what the Presbyterian Church
stands for, I want to become a member.
That is equivalent to the entire population of a city like Richmond, Virginia, or Lexington, Kentucky, or Tacoma, Washington.
More than a million children and adults had a
   solid church school curriculum, biblically based,
      to help them learn to live with integrity in this complex world.
What a miracle!
What marvelous things happen
   when you put that money in the plate.
What an amazing amount you get
   for the little you give.

As disciples of Jesus of Nazareth,
   sit down in these pews
   in companies of twenty and fifty this Sunday,
   and let me tell you three stories
      about bread,
   about your money,
      and bread.

First, let me put it in context.
We need to remember that
   the majority of our brothers and sisters

    live in huts made of mud and straw in this world,
  that the majority of our sisters and brothers
    go from one place to another on their own two feet
      or on backs of small beasts of burden,
  that the majority of our brothers and sisters in this world
    live and die without ever seeing a doctor or a nurse,
  that the majority of our sisters and brothers
    will go to bed tonight
      without having enough to eat.
But that is hard to grasp.
  Let me try it another way:
If the world were a global village of one hundred people,
  seventy of them would be unable to read,
  one would have a college education,
  more than fifty would be suffering from malnutrition,
  more than eighty would live in what we consider substandard housing.
Six of them would be Americans,
  and these six would have
    one-half of the village's entire income,
      and the other ninety-four would exist on the other half.

(At this point in the sermon I leave the pulpit, pick up a whole loaf of bread from the communion table, and tell the congregation that I would like them to think about bread as I tell them three stories. I ask them to pass the bread and take a piece, to look at it, to smell it, to taste it. Use a good whole wheat bread, and make sure you have enough. Sometimes I've used four loaves, each torn in half. I then walk up and down the center aisle and tell the stories.)

STORY 1

In Tanta, Egypt, I met a most unusual physician;
  his name is Dr. Alex Kahalil.

He is not only the chief surgeon but also the administrator of the
American Mission Hospital.
   It was established in 1892 by Presbyterians
      and has been sustained by our mission giving
         over all these years.
One day, we climbed into his ancient Volkswagen micro-bus
   and traveled way out into the Delta,
      to the farm of a rather wealthy artichoke grower.
About fifty people lived on the farm
   in mud huts.
They would never live any other place;
   they "belongèd" to the farm, and the owner
      turned out to be a benevolent man,
         who truly cared for these people.
I walked down the path between the huts and,
   about halfway down,
      my feet felt like they were pulling a ton of mud and manure.
A group of women were standing staring out at me
   and finally beckoned me to come in.
There were gathered there around an oven,
   baking the bread for the week.
I discovered that they baked the bread for a whole week,
   not because they liked stale bread,
      but because they conserved the wood they gathered for the fire.
         It was precious.
They tried to get me to make the bread,
   and I did my best.
It was like a pizza—I rolled it out fine,
   but, when I tried to throw it up in the air,
      it just came down in a gooey lump across my arm.
The women laughed,
   took it from me,

and deftly threw it into the oven.
　　It landed on a flat, hot rock,
　　　　sizzled,
　　and came out smelling and tasting wonderful.
They insisted I take it with me, and as I left,
　　I tried to refuse, to no avail.
I remember feeling like a Rockefeller;
　　that is how priceless that bread seemed to me.
And I got to thinking of all the work
　　that goes into so much of the world's bread.

STORY 2

A few weeks later I was in Beirut,
　　where I met some of your employees.
It was in the midst of the Lebanese civil war,
　　and our Jenishian Center,
　　　　established by Presbyterians long ago,
　　　　　　was reduced to helping people with the
　　　　　　　　truly bare necessities of life.
Of our fourteen mission workers there,
　　twelve had already sustained wounds from rifle fire or shrapnel.
They were reaching out and rescuing children
　　who were running alone through the streets,
　　　　and they tried to get them to their homes.
I remember how cold and drizzling the day was.
Out front there was a line of people
　　waiting to come to the door to receive
　　　　not bread, but a little sack of grain.
They would then take the grain home
　　and find some way to grind it into flour
　　　　so they could bake some bread.
That was how primitive things were

at that point in history.
Well, I saw a man in line who was missing a leg,
    and I asked, through an interpreter,
        if I could take his place.
So there I was,
    standing in the drizzle,
        cold,
            waiting my turn to get a little bag of grain.
I finally got it,
    gave it to the man,
        and asked for his forgiveness
            for the ostentatious life I lived.
I walked away, and I thought of
    all the bread I have wasted in my life,
        in restaurants and in my home.

STORY 3

A week later
    I found myself in an old, beat-up Chevrolet
        driving to Hebron in the occupied territories of Palestine.
At the wheel was one of your employees,
    Abdul Nassarin,
        an Arab Christian agricultural worker.
Your One Great Hour of Sharing offering
    makes possible his work,
        and his work was truly wonderful.
    He was teaching the farmers how to alternate olive trees with
    peach trees.
What I learned is that olive trees take about
    fourteen years to produce a crop,
        and, by that time, spread wide.

But local peach trees
   can produce a marketable crop in a couple of years,
      then can be cut down to allow the olive trees to spread.
We saw a man with a donkey and a plow.
   Abdul knew him and stopped the car.
Now, the land around Hebron is the rockiest land I have ever seen.
   The story goes that the devil and Gabriel had a rock fight there
      and then just left it.
This farmer had, as a plow, a shaft of steel with
   one little plow blade on it,
      connected to the donkey.
He was plowing furrows between rocks that were
   about sixteen inches apart.
Then he would bend over
   and go along the furrows
      and drop seed by hand.
All the searing summer long he would draw up water
   from a cistern,
      in a pitcher,
         and again bend over to water each row.
His hope was that the seed would germinate and grow
   and he could harvest wheat
      that he could then grind into flour
      and make bread.
Well, again, I asked through my friend
   if I could try that plowing,
      and I got all hitched up.
Well I don't know if the jackass was
   in front of the plow or behind it,
      but I just could not make that work.
It got to be lunch time,
   and the farmer asked us to walk to his house for something to eat.

We walked across those rocky fields
   and came to a small village.
All the houses were built of stone, and, because we were so "important,"
   he brought out a small table about a foot high
      and some cushions,
         and we sat in the street.
He then brought out
   a kettle of hot water for tea making
      and a loaf of bread,
         which he broke and gave to us.
And I thought of all the bent backs
   that are behind so much of the world's bread.

So:
Jesus said to the disciples
   "How much have you?"
      "Two fish and five loaves of bread."
And he took the fish and the bread and blessed it—
   broke it—
      and they (embarrassed at their selfishness)
         shared the bread
           and all ate and had enough.

Next week you will come before our God
   and declare what you will share—
      for the extended family
         in this place, and across the world.

Chapter 6

Aïda in the Bible

Set apart a tithe of all the yield of your seed that is brought in yearly from the field. In the presence of the LORD your God, in the place that he will choose as a dwelling for his name, you shall eat the tithe of your grain, your wine, and your oil, as well as the firstlings of your herd and flock, so that you may learn to fear the LORD your God always. But if, when the LORD your God has blessed you, the distance is so great that you are unable to transport it, because the place where the LORD your God will choose to set his name is too far away from you, then you may turn it into money. With the money secure in hand, go to the place that the LORD your God will choose; spend the money for whatever you wish—oxen, sheep, wine, strong drink, or whatever you desire. And you shall eat there in the presence of the LORD your God, you and your household rejoicing together. As for the Levites resident in your towns, do not neglect them, because they have no allotment or inheritance with you.

Every third year you shall bring out the full tithe of your produce for that year, and store it within your towns; the Levites, because they have no allotment or inheritance with you, as well as the resident aliens, the orphans, and the widows in your towns, may come and eat their fill so that the LORD your God may bless you in all the work that you undertake. —**Deut. 14:22–29**

Now concerning the collection for the saints: you should follow the directions I gave to the churches of Galatia. On the first day of every week, each of you is to put aside and save whatever extra you earn, so that collections need not be taken when I come. And when I arrive, I will send any whom

you approve with letters to take your gift to Jerusalem. If it seems advisable
that I should go also, they will accompany me. —1 Cor. 16:1–4

Let me begin today with a story from Rome,
    not ancient Rome,
        but contemporary Rome, a few years ago.
Just this fall,
    I heard a fascinating story about Clare Boothe Luce,
        who, you will remember, was once our ambassador to Italy.
It seems that she was living in a beautiful seventeenth-century Italian villa,
    but she soon began to notice that she was always tired.
        She lost weight;
            she seemed to have less and less energy.
She sought medical aid,
    and, after a period of intense testing,
        it was found that she was suffering from
            arsenic poisoning.
Everyone on her staff was given a security check,
    and it was soon established that everyone could be trusted.
None of her staff was trying to poison her,
    but where was the poisoning coming from?
Finally they found the cause.
    It was the ceiling of the bedroom.
There were beautiful designs of roses,
    ornately done in plaster relief,
        and they were painted with an old paint that contained
            arsenic lead.
A fine dust fell from the roses, and,
    completely unaware of what was happening,
        Mrs. Luce was slowly being poisoned in her bed
            from the fine dust falling from the ornate ceiling roses.

Similarly,
    completely unaware of what is happening,
        we are in danger of being poisoned
            by the ornate culture and society in which we live.
Our attitudes,
    concepts,
        values,
    can be eroded or poisoned by the materialistic values
        of those around us
            without our ever becoming aware of it
                until it is too late.
Without a doubt we live in the most acquisitive,
    consumer-oriented society
        the world has ever known!
Six thousand new products will be introduced to us this year alone,
    will vie for our dollars,
        and not one of the six thousand will be necessary for life,
            not even for the "full life."
But most of us will be persuaded to acquire
    at least some of them.
Who, who I ask you,
    really needs an electric toothpaste tube squeezer?
        Or a salad shooter, for that matter!
Is there any antidote,
    is there anything we can do
        to ward off the steady poisoning that we receive?

Let me tell you a true story. It was told to me by one of my colleagues in
Louisville, and it deeply affected and affects my life.
She told me how she left her Chinese student friend
    by the copy machine at the Presbyterian Center
        while she went to see a person in another office.
When she came back,

her friend was carefully stuffing an inch-thick wad
    of white paper into her tiny bag.
Her friend turned and said,
    "Someone threw this away."
After two months in this country,
    she was still shocked by our constant waste.
In her homeland, China, wood is rare and precious,
    so the white paper went home with us that day, said my friend.
The next morning my friend found the Chinese student
    carefully folding, cutting, and shaping the paper into envelopes.
      "I'm running out of them," she said.
Julia refrained from telling her
    that she could salvage half a dozen
      from the junk mail that would come in that day,
        and, instead, she lent her a glue stick.
That night, a pile of immaculate envelopes
    lay glued and carefully stacked on Julia's table.
"I didn't use your glue," her friend said.
    "It's expensive.
      I used the starch from the leftover noodles
        that stuck to the bottom of the pot,
          otherwise it would have been wasted."
That is one way to measure
    the gulf between us and most of the world,
      for most of the world shares her understanding
        of scarcity and make-do-ness.

Now let me deal with two passages of scripture
    that, perhaps, can give us some guidance,
      one from the Old Testament, one from the New.
In the book of Deuteronomy,
    we find that our mothers and fathers in the faith

not only knew how to
    diagnose and prescribe
    for this sickness,
  they were very blunt about it.
The basic teaching was
  God created all—
    sun, moon, stars,
    seas, lakes, mountains,
    iron ore, diamonds, plutonium,
    animals, birds, us.
  All is God's.
We use what is God's for a limited time.
  We are, as the scripture states,
    stewards—
      careful keepers and users
      of that which belongs to another.
To put structure around that concept,
  the law of Moses taught that the people must share
    so that all can benefit from the
      fabulous creation
        of this marvelous God.
What many do not realize
  is that they were expected not just to tithe,
    that is, to give one-tenth of their income,
  but to participate in
    three distinct tithes
    and, in addition, some special offerings, too.

The first tithe,
  known as the Lord's tithe,
  consisted of giving one-tenth annually
    of seed of the land,

of fruit of the tree,
    of herd of the flock.
The rationale was simple:
    "The earth is the LORD's, and the fullness thereof."
Therefore, since Yahweh was considered
    the owner of the land,
        it was only proper that Yahweh be given
            a share of its produce.
Most of this tithe
    went to support the Levites,
        who were the professional church staff of the day.
They were the ones who preached, taught, healed, helped, listened, and
led the celebrations.
In many respects this tithe corresponds to that part of
    a church's budget that goes to
        salaries and benefits of the staff.

The clergy staff:
    How do you put a price on pastoral ministry?
        On skills, energy, leadership,
        counseling, marriages, funerals, baptisms,
        preaching, teaching,
        encouraging you in your ministry,
        being a presence in the community?

The other professionals:
    How do you put a price on an excellent music program,
        on works of art magnificently performed to the glory of God?
        On the skillful work of staff with
            children,
            youth,
            and adults?

The support staff:
    Our business manager,
        who keeps all the work flowing,
        who comprehends the complex needs of our building and budget.
    Secretaries,
        enabling the professionals to respond to your needs,
        cranking out letters and communications,
        keeping us in touch with one another.
    Custodians,
        keeping our building clean and neat for our meetings and celebra
        tions and worship.
        Ever count the number of doors to be locked and opened?
        Ever count the window sills to be dusted?
        Ever count the chairs and tables to be moved?

The second tithe described in Deuteronomy
    paid for the travel and expense of the people
        during their stay in Jerusalem.
Three times a year, all the people went to Jerusalem—
    they were expected to gather there for
        Passover,
        the Feast of the Tabernacles,
        and the Feast of Weeks.
The second tithe was for payment for
    gathering the people for the ceremonies
        and for worship and decision making.
That correlates easily in our budget to the part that pays for
    the ways we gather here
        in committees,
        in session,
        in deacons,
    to discuss and plan,

to decide how to go into action.
It also goes for the per capita,
    that amount we send to presbytery, synod, and General Assembly
      to provide the structure of decision making
        on a representative, democratic basis,
        of which we, as Presbyterians, are so fond.
And it pays for our programs,
    programs that include
      adult education,
        education of our children and youth,
      travelers,
        pastoral visitors,
          the choirs,
        nine circles for our Presbyterian Women,
      Bible study, mission support, retreats,
        dinner forums,
          picnics,
            and softball.
It provides for this space,
    a place to gather to worship,
      as well as to study and enjoy one another in fellowship.
Everyone of us pays a bill for our own
    telephone, gas, electricity.
Ever consider what the church pays for these services
    so we can have a place to come and worship and learn?
Would you believe that at this church we pay . . .
    $6,000 for telephone,
    $11,000 for postage,
    $10,000 for insurance,
    $45,000 for gas and electricity,
      and
    over $4,000 just for cleaning supplies?

But there was a third tithe,
   given every three years,
      and kept in the local community
         for distribution to the needy.
Obviously, this correlates to our mission giving,
   those dollars that allow us to reach out to all the world,
      to touch, to lift, to heal, and to love.
And how much we do
   for the little we give!

In this community,
   we are reaching out to help
      the hungry and the homeless,
      the distressed and the unemployed.
And Alive, Alexandria Hospital,
   the bag lunch program, Bethany House,
      Carpenter's Shelter, Christmas in April,
         the domestic violence program,
            the emergency relief assistance fund.
And the George Mason School project, Good News Mission,
   Guest House, Habitat for Humanity, Hospice of North Virginia,
   Martha's Table, Meals on Wheels,
      network preschool,
         Residential Youth Services,
           So Others Might Eat,
              Untouchables.
Just pick one—
   like Carpenter's Shelter—
      beyond all the hours given
         by members of Westminster who provide meals,
      we give more than $8,000 each year for expenses.
But that is a drop in the bucket when it comes to the need.

Carpenter's Shelter pays $14,000 a month
    for the facility—
        but that facility provided more than forty thousand bed nights last
        year
            for the homeless of our community.
But more—
    It provided comprehensive case management systems,
        hot meals,
            clean linen,
                the opportunity to take a shower
                    and launder clothes.
I haven't mentioned the hundreds of "overflow" people
    who come through the facility in the really bad weather.

Through our presbytery,
    we reach out and touch more than a million people each year,
        in day centers and night shelters,
        in youth ministry,
        through ministry to the homeless.
    We are helping to
        keep open strategic congregations in changing neighborhoods.

Through the Synod of the Mid-Atlantic,
    we are helping provide ministries at more than fifty campuses,
    a home for orphans, runaways, and victims of child abuse,
    training for clergy and lay
        in the areas of youth work and Christian education.

Through our General Assembly,
    we reach out to brothers and sisters in seventy-nine nations on five
    continents,
        where more than two million people will receive

   hospital and medical care, where no alternatives are available,
  where agricultural and educational experts will
   help establish good farms, nutrition programs, and schools for
   countless others.
We support strategically located congregations in rural areas of the United
States,
  develop mass media presentations,
  and produce a curriculum
   that effectively educates our 1.5 million children.

Wow! How much we do
  for the little we give!
How much more we will be able to do
  with our increased giving this next year!

Counting the first two annual tithes
  and the three-year tithe,
   a conscientious Jew gave about
     23.33 percent of the family income,
  and, in addition, gave to special, free will offerings throughout the year!
And they were joyful about it . . .
  They did not see it as anything other than an opportunity to rejoice.
They had their priorities straight; they were, in the words of Paul,
  hilarious givers!
For the earth, the whole earth,
  is God's, and the fullness thereof.
Talk about giving
  hilariously and celebratively,
   listen to this description in the book of Numbers
    of what happened
     when the tabernacle was consecrated:
The leaders of the tribes of Israel, on their own initiative,

brought gifts to take care of transporting the tabernacle
    and to provide for the rituals.
Their spontaneous and generous stewardship
    was an example to Israel for every age,
        and it could well be for us today.
It's a long description of the
    leaders' dedication and generosity.
It went on for twelve days—
    count them—twelve days!
Offerings of gold, silver vessels,
    fine flour, oil, incense,
    rams, oxen, lambs, and goats.
For twelve days, they processed up to the tabernacle,
    carrying their symbols of dedication.
It must have looked like the grand entrance scene from Aïda !

> The one who presented his offering the first day was Nahshon son
> of Amminadab, of the tribe of Judah. His offering was one silver
> plate weighing one hundred thirty shekels, one silver basin weigh-
> ing seventy shekels . . . both of them full of choice flour mixed with
> oil for a grain offering; one golden dish weighing ten shekels, full
> of incense; one young bull, one ram, one male lamb a year old, for
> a burnt offering; one male goat for a sin offering; and for the sacri-
> fice of well-being, two oxen, five rams, five male goats, and five
> male lambs a year old. This was the offering of Nahshon son of Am-
> minadab. (Num. 7:12–17)

And it went on:
    eleven tribes took their turn!

They brought their offerings willingly,
    thanking Yahweh, who had been so good to them,
        who had brought them out of slavery in Egypt,

led them through the wilderness,
    provided for them in all their needs.
So they dedicated their
    time and talents and treasures to this Yahweh,
        who had so visibly loved them.
It was a time of dedication
    and commitment.

But now let me turn to a New Testament text:
All of us have heard the magnificent fifteenth chapter of
    Paul's first letter to the Corinthians.
He takes off and soars,
    talking of eternal life!
"Listen, and I will tell you a secret," he says.
    "We shall not all die,
    but suddenly, in a twinkling of an eye,
    everyone will be changed as the trumpet sounds.
    Death is swallowed up in victory:
        Where O death is your power to hurt us?
        Where O grave is the victory you hope to win?
    Thanks be to God who gives us the victory over these things
        through our Lord Jesus Christ!"
And then Paul abruptly makes a shift,
    or so it seems,
    for almost in the same breath he says,
"Now about the collection for the saints. . . .
    Every Sunday each of you is to put aside and keep
        by you a sum in proportion to your gain . . . "
That, you see, is Paul's logic;
    nothing is more typical of him than this.
He has been walking in the lofty realms of theology,
    discussing life in the world to come, and
        then zap! He begins to deal with the here and now.

Once and for all, Paul announced that the
    resurrection and the offering
        belong together!
The news has not penetrated to some,
    but without giving,
        there is an unfinished resurrection.
Putting something aside as a habit means
    setting our priorities straight,
        getting into a larger world,
            into Yahweh's time and space,
                where the whole family lives.
John Calvin, our touchstone in the Reformed family,
    taught that material goods are instruments of God.
Money becomes the means God uses to help persons.
So God puts wealth at our disposal . . .
    —so that we may organize our life and the life of our community
    —to bring shalom, the fullest possible, sustainable life for all persons
    everywhere
    —to organize the society in which we live in a responsible way, in sol-
    idarity with all others.
But Calvin also warned that the devil brings sin among us,
    and we become selfish and ingrown
        and try to insulate and isolate ourselves
            from the community.
Thereby, we negate the good values of our money.
We then come to idolize our money
    and give it a place it should not have,
        so that it becomes divine
            and has power over us.
The devil, claim scripture and Calvin,
    seductively leads us to say,
        "After all, it's my money,
            not God's,

that assures my daily bread
  and guarantees my future."

John Updike wrote a short story titled "The Wallet."
It's about Fulham, a retired broker, "who had assembled a nice life after
thirty years of marriage, a handsome white house in the older suburbs."
Fulham spends his time managing his own investments
    and those of a favored few long-time clients
        from an upstairs room in his house.
Every morning he goes to his room
    with the *Wall Street Journal,*
        a second cup of decaffeinated coffee,
            and makes some phone calls.
    As he does, he looks out the window at his
        neatly manicured lawn
            and surveys and enjoys the world he has gained.
Then disaster strikes.
    One morning he can't find his wallet.
Now, if you are not a compulsive, obsessive person,
    you may not understand what this story is about.
If you are, if you spend as much time as I do
    in a state of agitation because you can't find your keys or your pen,
        then you may find it funny and provocative.
Fulham looks everywhere—
    under chairs, beds,
        he even goes through pockets of suits he hasn't worn for months.
He goes a little berserk.
    His wallet was "a friendly adjunct to his person,
        a reminder, in its delicate pressure upon his left buttock
        of his new stage of life
        containing charge cards for
            Bay Bank, Brooks Brothers, Hertz, American Express
        plus his plasticized driver's license

and cards signifying his membership in the
    country club, Museum of Fine Arts, and Social Security,
       and pictures of his kids."
After several days of searching,
  Fulham, punctuating his proclamation with obscenities,
    announces to his wife
    that someone, obviously, has slipped into the house
      and stolen the wallet.

      His wife says, "I've never seen you like this."
      Fulham asks, "How am I?"
      Wife: "You're wild."
      Fulham: "It was my wallet. Everything is in it. Everything.
      Without that wallet, I'm nothing."

Fulham finds his wallet,
  in fact his grandson finds it folded up in a blanket on the
couch.
And Updike closes with him "squeezing the beloved bent book of
leather
  between his two palms
    and feeling very grand, paternal, fragile, wiser, and
    ready to die."
"Without that wallet, I'm nothing," Fulham said . . .

Jesus said,
  "What shall it profit a person to gain the whole world
  and to forfeit his or her life?"
So it is very clear that the Bible
  and Paul
    and Calvin

Are saying to us that we need consciously
   to dethrone money
      and to see it in its proper perspective and context.
By taking our money
   and bringing it before our Lord,
      dedicating it to the use of the
         expansion of the kingdom of God,
            our creator and sustainer,
   we thereby assert
      that it does not have a divine hold on us,
      that we belong to one that is above the money,
         a universal provider,
         who provides through all the bulls and bears,
         who provides where neither moth nor rust consumes,
            and where no thief can break in and steal.
So, we can assure our continued freedom
   not to become slaves to mammon—our money—
   but, rather, to live as people devoted to God
      using all that God has given us
         to extend his blessings to others.
For money is another
   pair of legs,
      and it can go places we could never go
      and do all sorts of things we could never do!

Today, you will be asked to bring your pledge
   to the front of the sanctuary,
      to the communion table,
         in an act of dedication and commitment.
   It will be your decision not to be a slave
      to the material, acquisitive, consumer society,

but to be a part of the body of Christ throughout the world
    to give legs,
    and arms,
    and mouth,
       to the Christ—
to bring about a measure of shalom
    as this family reaches out
       to touch, to lift, to heal, to love
in the name of Jesus,
    who frees us
       and keeps us free.

And now, with apologies to William Shakespeare:

To pledge, or not to pledge,
    that is the question.
Whether 'tis nobler in a man
    to take the gospel free
    and let the other fellow foot the bill,
Or sign a pledge and pay toward church expenses!
To give, to pay—aye, there's the rub. To pay,
    when on the free-pew plan, a man may have a sitting free and take the
    gospel too,
    as though he paid,
    and none be aught the wiser.
To err is human, and human too,
    to buy at cheapest rate.
I'll take the gospel so!
    For others do the same—a common rule!
I'm wise.
    I'll wait, not work.

I'll pray, not pay.
And let the other fellow foot the bill,
    and so I'll get the gospel free, you see!

But there is no cheap grace—
    it cost God his son.

Chapter 7

Keeper of the Pig Sty

You are the salt of the earth; but if salt has lost its taste, how can its salti-
ness be restored? It is no longer good for anything, but is thrown out and
trampled under foot.

You are the light of the world. A city built on a hill cannot be hid. No one
after lighting a lamp puts it under the bushel basket, but on the lampstand,
and it gives light to all in the house. In the same way, let your light shine
before others, so that they may see your good works and give glory to your
*Father in heaven. —**Matt. 5:13–16***

Do I need to tell you that today is "Pledge Sunday"?
    You all know that.
    You all know what I'm going to say.
"He's going to ask me for money.
    He's going to try to make me feel stingy.
       But I've already made up my mind what I'm going to give."
Is that in your mind?
    You are not alone, then.
Philadelphia's own venerable Ben Franklin
    thought the same thing many years ago.
In his autobiography, he tells of how he went to church one day,
    and these are Ben's own words:

> I perceived the pastor intended to finish with a collection, and I si-
> lently resolved he should get nothing from me. I had, in my pocket,
> a handful of copper money, three or four silver dollars, and five gold

pieces. As he proceeded I began to soften, and concluded to give the
coppers. Another stroke of his oratory made me ashamed of that, and
I determined to give the silver. And he finished so admirably, that I
emptied my pocket wholly into the collector's dish, gold and all.

Well I had a problem even before that,
  namely, how to get people to come this Sunday at all.
So, I quietly resolved to try to persuade people to come this Sunday
  by coming up with a creative,
    outrageous title:
      "Keeper of the Pig Sty."
But having raised your curiosity,
  what in the world will I do with the title now?
Ah ha!
  You thought I didn't have a plan?
Well, it all has to do with the very word
  "stewardship."
You see, when you break it down, you discover
  that it is a combination of the words
    "sty" and "ward."
  "Ward" is defined as "one who guards."
  "Sty" is defined as "a pen or enclosure for swine, pigs."
As a matter of fact,
  in jolly old England a few centuries ago,
    one of the most important offices was that of steward.
Coming originally from a time when the
  steward had general control of managing the affairs of the
    medieval household and estate,
  a steward came to be an officer in the empire,
    again with responsibility to manage the affairs of the land.
So they are fine words—"steward" and "stewardship"—
  defining first a person
    who kept pigs for someone else.

They were not his pigs,
  but he was responsible for their well-being,
    their increase.
The term "steward" gradually came to mean generally
  one who manages another's property, finances, or other affairs.
Well now, there you have it.

Let me give you our theology of stewardship
  in a capsule:
We can say most of the verses by heart:

1. In the beginning God created the heavens and the earth.
2. And the Lord God planted a garden in Eden.
3. And the Lord God took the human he had made
   and put the human in the garden
       to keep it and to till it.

And keep it and till it we have done,
  and we have done very well with it,
    and the good land that always belongs to God
      has produced prodigiously for us.

Listen to this from Deuteronomy:

> Take care you do not forget Yahweh your God. . . . When you have
> eaten and had all you want, when you have built fine houses to live
> in, when you have seen your flocks and herds increase, your silver
> and gold abound, and all your possessions grow great—do not be-
> come proud of heart. Do not then forget Yahweh your God—who
> brought you out of the land of Egypt, out of the house of slavery:
> who guided you through this vast and dreadful wilderness, a land
> of fiery serpents, scorpions, thirst; who in this waterless place
> brought you water from the hardest rock; who in this wilderness fed
> you with manna. . . . Beware of saying in your heart, "My own
> strength and the might of my own hand won this power for me."

Remember Yahweh your God: it was he who gave you this strength
and won you this power. (Deut. 8:11–18, Jerusalem Bible)

Be sure, therefore, that you do not forget Yahweh your God.

And, in the words of Psalm 24:1,

The earth is the LORD's, and the fullness thereof;
the world, and all who dwell therein.

Oh my, how tempted we are,
    when the stock market continues to rise,
        to think that it is all somehow our own doing,
            our own cleverness, that we have today
    more disposable income per household
        than ever in the history of our nation.
So we then assume that, because we have this disposable income,
    this income above and beyond the amount that is necessary for life,
        we must dispose of it.

And dispose of it we do . . .
Our problem today
    is that our net income
        doesn't keep up
            with our gross habits.
And our gross habits are the result
    of a society prone to be led into more and more materialism.
How often we read these days
    about the effect of advertising
        on the lifestyle of us all.
I used to love to read to the kids, when they were growing up,
    some of the tales from the *Arabian Nights* collection.
I remember one where a person was effectively put to death
    by an ingenious method.

The perpetrator noted that the victim was an avid reader
   and that the reader licked his fingers
      each time he turned the page of the book.
So the evil one put arsenic on the page tops,
   and the reader slowly and effectively poisoned himself
      each time he licked his finger and turned a page.
I get that image in my mind
   as I see the subtle, yet continuous, ways
      that our society influences us
         to use more and more of our disposable income
            for those things far above "necessities."
Then we say we can't afford any more for the church,
   can't give any more of our increase back to God.

Well, that's a lot of heavy stuff—
   so time for some stories instead:

(At this point in the sermon, I went out of the pulpit and told stories as I walked about. I also called on two members of the congregation to tell a story each.)

At a church meeting,
   a very wealthy man
      rose to tell the rest of those present
         about his Christian faith.

         "I am a millionaire," he said,
            "and I attribute it all to the rich blessings of God in my life.
         I remember the turning point in my faith.
            I had just earned my first dollar,
               and I went to a church meeting that night.
         The speaker was a missionary
            who told about his work.

I knew that I only had a dollar bill
    and had to either give it all to God's work
        or nothing at all!
So at that moment,
    I decided to give my whole dollar—everything I had—
to God.
    I believe that God blessed that decision,
        and that is why I am a rich man today."

He finished, and there was an awed silence
    at his testimony
        as he moved toward his seat.
As he sat down,
    a little old lady sitting in the same pew leaned over to him and said,
        "I dare you to do it again."

Henri Rush—
    you are one of our elders—
        tell us a story of our disposable income
            making a difference in Kinshasa.

(He told about our relationship to a congregation in Africa and of his trip
to formalize our relationship.)

Here is a story about a man sitting in the pew when
    the plate was passed to collect money for such a project as Henri
    described.
When the usher put the plate before the man, he politely declined to put
anything in.
The usher pushed it at him again, and the man said,

        "I don't believe in foreign missions."
    The usher pushed it at him again and said,
        "Then take some out—it's for the heathen."

Kris Abrahamsen—
  you are one of our deacons—
    and you can tell a mission story.

(She told a story about our Habitat for Humanity project.)

This summer in Alaska, Kay and I heard the following story:
Two guys were going on a moose hunt and contacted a local bush pilot
  to take them to their favorite lake.
They made the deal,
  loaded the plane with all the stuff they needed for a two-week stay,
    and off they went.

        As they approached the lake, the pilot said,
          "I can't land on a lake that small."
        One of the hunters said, "Well, the pilot last year did."
        "Well, OK," said the pilot, and land he did—but it took
        most of the lake to do it.
        He unloaded the two hunters,
          all their gear, and said, "See you in two weeks."
        In two weeks, the plane came back,
          landed, and there were the two hunters, their gear, and
        two moose.
        "Wait a minute," said the pilot,
          "I will not be able to take off with that load."
        "Well," said one of the hunters,
          "we did last year."
        "Well, OK."

So the pilot took the plane to the far edge of the lake,
  revved up the engine to full speed,
    raced down the lake,
      and just as he was about to run out of lake,
        lifted off.

He skimmed the trees at the edge of the lake,
    then crashed.
The three of them crawled out of the wreck,
    and the pilot said,

                "I thought you said you did it last year—
                    do you see where we are?"
            "Yep, about a mile farther this year."

Folks—friends of Westminster Presbyterian Church—
    a mile better than last year
        is not enough.
In our scripture of the morning,
    Jesus gives us our goal,
        gives us our marching orders:
    You are the salt of the earth;
        you are the light of the world.

There is a new pastor coming;
    you are about to step across a threshold
        into a wondrous future.
There are new programs
        waiting to be born;
    there are calls to participate in new mission,
        both in Alexandria and in the world.
And all this will be stillborn
    unless you support it
        with your pledge today
            and your money tomorrow.
You hold the key.
In a few minutes you will come forward
    and present your intentions for the coming year.

But before that happens,
    I ask you to take a few minutes to meditate in silence,
        perhaps to reconsider your decision
            as to how much you will pledge
                to permit Westminster to cross that threshold
                    into a new, even more vibrant future.

PART THREE

ENDOWMENTS

Chapter 8

Creative Use of Congregational Endowments

A bit of history . . .

During the first half of my ministry, I heard pastors say—almost universally—that an endowment was a bad thing for a congregation. Now we did, in those years, have some congregations with endowments. Growing up in Pittsburgh, I always heard about "Mellon's Fire Escape," that magnificent Presbyterian church that looks like a gothic cathedral sitting in the middle of the East Liberty section of the city. Mellon, banker that he was, not only built that structure but endowed it.

There were others, of course, and often it was said that those congregations never did have to know anything about stewardship or even about just giving to the budget. They "had it made." What the pastors often meant was that they did not feel that they had to talk about stewardship, and some of them truly could, when the budget came up with a deficit, walk down the street, or make a couple of calls, and get the money necessary to balance the budget.

But, gradually, some of us took issue with this kind of thinking. After all, we had all been solicited by our colleges to build the endowments of those institutions. So bit by bit—and with little or no encouragement or help from the denomination—we set out to do a little endowment building.

Sometime in 1985, a group of us who were pastors of congregations that had, by that time, significant endowments informally got together to talk about the effect of endowments on congregations. Eventually, with the help of the Lilly Foundation, we gathered representatives of thirty-eight Presbyterian congregations who had "significant endowments" to share their special concerns and needs. As I remember it, we took the only source we had, the statistical part of the General Assembly Minutes (which are never complete in the column of "endowments"), and sent letters to any that had endowments over $1.5 million. About 120 letters were sent.

Tom Stewart, pastor of Westminster Presbyterian Church in Buffalo, served as convener. Loren B. Mead, director of the Alban Institute, served as consultant, and Robert Lynn, senior vice president of the Lilly Endowment, was our major speaker.

Looking back on that time just a dozen years ago, I see that we were quite timid. Few people were willing to really come out and talk about money in the church, and fewer still about endowments. So we agreed (according to Loren Mead's report) to "Four Guiding Principles":

1. Confidentiality: that we would speak as directly as we could of things that are generally not spoken about in church circles, and we would trust each other to use what we learned responsibly.
2. Risk: that we recognized and were willing to accept the fact that to speak of what we were to speak of—even to come to this meeting itself—involved a risk of taking a leadership role.
3. Stewardship: that our interest was in being better stewards of the resources God had given us to care for—and that this concern was the central issue that brought us together, a matter of faith, commitment, and responsibility.
4. Loyalty: that everything we were doing was done on the basis of our full loyalty to our Presbyterian heritage and within Presbyterian structures.

Gathering in small groups, we came up with a series of issues that we wanted to explore. These became the continuing agenda of yearly gatherings that followed and were the *raison d'être* for the formation of the current "National Association of Presbyterian Endowed Congregations."

THE MAIN ISSUES

STEWARDSHIP ISSUES:

- How to educate about stewardship, especially how to differentiate annual giving from estate planning and endowment development.

THEOLOGICAL ISSUES:

- What does it mean to be a rich congregation in a poor world?
- What are the mission implications for congregations with large resources?
- How does "social responsibility" fit into how we manage our resources?
- How does a "wealthy" church develop a theological vision?
- What is the role of endowment in a congregation that is "dying"?
- Is "invading" the principal an issue of morality?

MANAGEMENT AND CONTROL ISSUES:

- What do you disclose and to whom?
- Are there appropriate levels of disclosure?
- How do you separate the functions of "trustee" and "session"?
- Who does long-range planning?
- How is the pastor involved with the control of the funds?

TECHNICAL ISSUES:

- How do you determine whether to seek investment strategies for growth or income?
- How much risk is appropriate?

- What does "principal" mean and how do you responsibly keep track of it?
- How do you define "corpus"?
- What divisions of responsibility make sense?
- How do you go about soliciting new endowments?

CONGREGATIONAL ISSUES:

- How does the use of the endowment relate to that congregation's sense of mission?
- How does that congregation live with its community (secular and ecclesiastical) with its "image" as a wealthy church?
- How do you balance discipline with vision in the use of funds?
- How can dollars challenge the sense of ministry "for" as opposed to ministry "to"?
- What do we do about responsibility for mission beyond the congregation?
- How do you set stewardship goals for the endowment (the way you set investment goals, for example)?
- How does the church stay responsible to the intent of the donor of the funds?
- How do you get diverse groups involved in decision making about use of the endowment income?
- How do Presbyterian congregations express their polity in their relationship to their endowments?

THE PRESBYTERIAN FOUNDATION

A lot of water has gone over the dam since that initial meeting. The group formed the National Association of Endowed Presbyterian Churches and, what is more significant, the Presbyterian Foundation was approached and became an active partner. In a few years, the foundation put in place excellent materials to assist congregations with developing endowments. In addition, it has done a stellar job in training its field directors to work with presbyteries and congregations in this field.

OVER THE YEARS STUDIES HAVE INDICATED:

1. Creating and growing an endowment does not adversely affect the annual budget funding campaign of a congregation provided that there is full disclosure of the endowment—full disclosure. It seems essential that every year the congregation receive a detailed report of how much is in the fund, by category or designated fund, how much it earned, and how it was used.
2. The endowment will grow if members can see that the money is used and not just "socked away."
3. Therefore, the session should clearly outline the purpose of the endowment. That purpose varies widely across the denomination.
4. The wisest decision is to place endowment funds with the Presbyterian Foundation for management. Not only is this often cost-effective and the return substantial, it removes from the congregation members the possibility of criticizing some of its own "financial" people, who would otherwise have to make such decisions.
5. Each time the endowment is used, the purpose and the result should be publicized to the congregation. Again, the more the congregation sees that the endowment is effectively used for a variety of purposes, the more will be contributed.

SOME CREATIVE USES:

A couple years ago I did a nationwide phone survey and discovered a wide range of creative uses of endowments.

> A well-endowed upper-class church in the East made a grant
> to a black Baptist church so they could fix their leaking

sanctuary windows. They also gave a significant grant to another small church for rebuilding after it had been partially destroyed by arson.

A congregation in a changing neighborhood has used its endowment to construct a homeless shelter in its area and to fund an interfaith council for the homeless.

A congregation in a wealthy suburb makes available college scholarships for children in three very poor sections of a metropolitan area. They also funded a Planned Parenthood clinic in one of these areas.

One congregation used part of its endowment each year to bring a third-world pastor or scholar to work in the church for a two- or three-week period, in order to sensitize the congregation to different lifestyles and cultures.

A Midwest congregation used part of its endowment to build a public swimming pool for a part of the community, consisting of low-income housing, and to underwrite a food program that distributed bags of food once a week.

A downtown congregation used its endowment to establish a new position on the church staff to work in urban ministry. No "in-house" duties were assigned this person, only work in the community on its issues and problems.

Another congregation used part of its endowment to set up a memorial lectureship honoring a former pastor, who had been very progressive in his leadership. They bring an outstanding speaker to the community each year, some internationally known.

One congregation uses its endowment to guarantee loans obtained by various community groups working on social problems.

Money was sent to restore church buildings damaged by the

California earthquake and some funds were allocated to establish a library in Zaire and a medical mission in Korea.

Realizing that a growing number of older parishioners had health needs, one congregation used a part of its endowment to put a nurse on its staff. She moves about the parish visiting, taking blood pressure, coordinating medical visits, explaining medication to the homebound, responding to calls to distant relatives, and giving educational seminars on AIDS and other diseases.

A congregation in the West was dropping in its membership, attendance, and program. A significant part of its endowment was used to move quickly into new programs and outreach. It turned the congregation around, the average age falling dramatically from sixty-eight to forty-three. Income doubled, and strategic programs to continue to reach people not now in the church are bringing in a new day of life and service.

On the other coast, a historic downtown church used part of its endowment to fund a creative advertising campaign. They used billboards and imaginative ads on the fine arts radio station to turn around a dwindling membership.

One congregation in the West discovered that children who were abused were being warehoused and dumped in overcrowded, impersonal facilities. They used endowment funds to create a program involving forty congregations to provide Christian foster homes, where children who were damaged are given a new lease on life.

A medical school was near a certain congregation in a metropolitan area with great need surrounding it. The congregation used endowment funds to enable medical students to serve in public health ministries in the city.

Seeing great needs in a metropolitan community, one congregation set up a special fund that could be used by members of the congregation who were themselves involved in some project. But members had to be there with sleeves rolled up, willing to come back and educate the congregation about the causes of urban problems. Among other things, they set up a cleaning business where employees can build up a good record of attendance, attitude, and initiative and can learn good interview skills and how to write resumes. People who had not been able to get good jobs were enabled to secure permanent employment.

Another endowment fund is used to make grants to students from the congregation and presbytery for theological education. Twenty students are currently receiving such funds.

And sometimes these creative ideas do not work! One congregation used funds to renovate an old building, put in a service for the mentally disabled, and maintain it, along with a grocery store and laundromat on the first floor—but it failed. On the positive side, this congregation gives more than $40,000 in college scholarships each year to an adolescent alcohol and drug addiction program.

The point is clear. Congregations can get excited about gathering and using these kinds of funds.

So . . .

1. Don't hoard it.
2. Don't spend it on luxuries.
3. Don't use it as an excuse—to retire from the duties of congregational life.

Instead . . .

1. Use it for the sake of others.
2. Tell people about it.
3. Use it to accomplish things that otherwise might not get done.

And above all remember . . .

> The earth is the Lord's, and the fullness thereof;
> the world and all who dwell therein.

Chapter 9

"The Ultimate Fool"

Someone in the crowd said to him, "Teacher, tell my brother to divide the family inheritance with me." But he said to him, "Friend, who set me to be a judge or arbitrator over you?" And he said to them, "Take care! Be on your guard against all kinds of greed; for one's life does not consist in the abundance of possessions." Then he told them a parable: "The land of a rich man produced abundantly. And he thought to himself, 'What should I do, for I have no place to store my crops?' Then he said, 'I will do this: I will pull down my barns and build larger ones, and there I will store all my grain and my goods. And I will say to my soul, 'Soul, you have ample good laid up for many years; relax, eat, drink, be merry.' But God said to him, 'You fool! This very night your life is being demanded of you. And the things you have prepared, whose will they be?' So it is with those who store up treasures for themselves but are not rich toward God. —Luke 12:13–21

I grew up in Pittsburgh.
You can make two rather sure assumptions about people of my age who grew up in Pittsburgh:

    1. If you are a Protestant, you are almost surely a Presbyterian.
    2. You know the story of Andrew Carnegie.

From my mother's knee,
  in school,
    and through many institutions in the city,
  I learned that Carnegie

came to America from Scotland in 1848,
　that his first job was as a bobbin boy in a textile mill,
　that he went on to jobs in a
　　telegraph office,
　　　in railroads,
　　　　and eventually in iron ore and steel.
We actually breathed the lore of Andrew Carnegie
　when I was growing up,
　　every soot-filled morning,
　　　every dreary smoke-darkened day.
I spent one summer
　carrying fire brick
　　to men who were relining a Carnegie blast furnace,
　　and it was in the midst of that gritty, grimy, sweat-filled summer
　　　that I decided to go to college.
Now most of us also knew
　that our great benefactor
　　was a robber baron par excellence.
My folks and my friends' parents
　told the stories of how he grew Carnegie Steel
　　into the biggest American steel producer in the world
　　　partly through
　　　　intimidation and other unsavory tactics.
But we also knew that much of our
　cultural and educational life
　　was due to the way he saw his wealth—
　a perspective that came from being an
　　active Presbyterian.
In an 1889 article he wrote, "There are but three modes in which surplus
wealth can be disposed of. It can be left to the families of the decedents; or
it can be bequeathed for public purposes; or, finally, it can be administered
by its possessors during their lives."

Obviously, he worked at the third option,
    donating $350 million in his lifetime,
        which is equivalent to $5.4 billion today!
His specialty, as we all know,
    was libraries.
When he started, there were nine hundred libraries in the whole country.
    With his leadership twenty-five hundred more came into existence,
        and what a difference that made in the fabric of our society.
I still remember one of his maxims:
    "The man who dies rich—dies disgraced."
None of us falls into Carnegie's category,
    but we have a lot of potential Carnegies around.
I wish they would take notice of
    Oseola McCarty,
        an eighty-seven-year-old Mississippi woman
            who recently gave a hefty grant to fund
                scholarships for black students
            at the University of Southern Mississippi.
The amount she gave, $150,000,
    is a pittance to some of the biggies in our society today,
        but she puts them to shame.
    She donated her entire life savings,
        earned over decades of washing richer people's clothes.

So with that in the background,
    now we come to our first biblical text of the day.
One of the main themes of the Old Testament is
    to leave what you have,
        to free yourself from all fetters,
            to simply be.
The history of our faith family begins with the command to its first heroes,
    Sarah and Abraham,

to give up their country, their clan, their friends
and to go—
"Go," said Yahweh, "from your kindred and your father's house to the
land I will show you."
Leave what you have and
be on an adventure to the unknown.
And so the story begins:
They walk a thousand miles to the land of Canaan,
then ultimately to Egypt.
They settle down in Egypt,
and they become rich and powerful in Egypt.
Scripture says,

> From Egypt, Abram returned to the Negev with his wife and all he
> possessed and Lot with him. Abram was a very rich man with live-
> stock, silver and gold. (Gen. 13:1–2, Jerusalem Bible)

But then their descendants return and settle down in Egypt,
and Joseph leads them into an age of
unprecedented wealth and power.
Joseph was clever, quick, perceptive, imaginative—
a dreamer, but more than a dreamer—
a man with the creative ability to interpret complex phenomena,
to forecast and foresee,
to plan and administer.
Quiet, industrious, able in all economic and financial affairs,
he knew well how to serve power and
exploit it on behalf of his people.
As Pharaoh said to him,
"There is none so discreet and wise as you" (Gen. 41:39).

And a new clannishness developed,
an elitism born of the success of Joseph and his descendants.

But after four hundred years,
   "a pharaoh arose who knew not Joseph."
Precisely because they had become rich and powerful in Egypt,
    they became slaves, and they lost the
      vision of the God, Yahweh,
        who had spoken so effectively to Sarah and Abraham.
And they began to worship idols,
    the gods of the rich—
They become enslaved because,
    instead of the God who is free and transcendent and not able to be possessed,
      they turn to idols,
        which can be possessed,
          and it leads to their slavery.
But a second set of heroes comes on the scene.[1]
Moses and Miriam are charged by Yahweh
    to liberate the people again,
      to lead them out from the country that has become their home,
        and to go into the desert.
Reluctantly and with great misgiving,
    they follow their leaders into the desert.
The desert is the key symbol of the liberation.
    The desert is no home,
      it has no cities,
        it has no riches.
It is a place of nomads who
    own what they need,
      and what they need are the necessities of life,
        not possessions.

---

[1]I am indebted for some of the insights in this section to Erich Fromm's book *To Have or to Be*, New York: Harper & Row, 1976.

So they live with the bread of the wanderer—unleavened bread—
    and the tents of a wanderer, easily built and easily taken down.
And through it all,
    there is the whining of some
        to go back to the fleshpots of Egypt,
            to go back to the certainties,
                to go back to slavery.
In the midst of the exodus,
    there is another lesson to be learned,
        and it has to do with food.
God promises to feed them on this trip,
    and in the morning he gives them bread
        and in the evening quail.
But God adds two important injunctions:
    1. They are to gather only what they need.
    2. And the second, a corollary, is an injunction against hoarding, greed,
    and possessiveness.
They were enjoined not to save anything for the next day.
    But they didn't listen to Moses,
        and when they tried to hoard the food,
            it bred worms overnight and the next day became foul.
This becomes a symbol of what really happens
    to the people of Israel
        in the wilderness.
For the story has a very sad end:
    the people cannot bear to live without having,
        cannot bear to live without possessing,
            cannot bear to live without some visible, tangible thing.
And you know how the story goes:
Moses disappears on the mountain
    to receive the Ten Commandments,
        and the frightened, desperate people

convince Aaron to make them a
visible manifestation
of something that they can worship:
a golden calf.
It was something they could see,
something they could hold onto,
something they could possess,
something they could have.
And this sin
causes a whole generation to perish in the wilderness
before the new generation can attain the Promised Land.
But even after they conquer it
and possess it under Joshua,
it becomes clear that they have not learned the lesson,
for they transform their democratic tribal life
into an oriental despotism
and settle down
again to be possessed by their possessions.
It fell to the prophets
to take up again
the task to renew the vision of human freedom,
of being unfettered by things.
Amos railed against those who had
winter and summer homes,
silk upholstery,
ivory objets d'art.
Still the people would not listen.
They continued to be idolatrously fixated
on the land,
on their possessions.
They were incapable of living as free people.
And so another lesson was given to them:

They were removed from the land in the exile,
   forced once more to be
     free from possessions,
   forced once more to
     discover the God who cannot be possessed,
   forced once more into a
     "being" form of living
       instead of a "having" form of living.
But it did not last.
A few centuries later,
   Jesus comes on the scene with the vision
     of freedom once again.
The Sermon on the Mount is a radical restatement
   of the teaching of Yahweh
     that the people must free themselves—
       free themselves from all greed
         and the cravings for possessions.
   They must be totally liberated from the structures of having.
Jesus taught:

> Do not store up for yourselves treasures on earth where moth and rust consume and where thieves break in and steal; but store up for yourselves treasures in heaven, where neither moth nor rust consumes and where thieves do not break in and steal. For where your treasure is, there your heart will be also. (Matt. 6:19–21)

One of the truly frightening things of our day
   is the recognition that we live in a society
     that rests on the pillars of
       property, profit, and power
         for its existence.
To acquire,
   to own,

     to make a profit
  are the sacred and unalienable rights of our society.
What the sources of property are does not matter.
Nor does possession impose any obligations on property owners.

My word, I remember that my grandfather
  had a little bit of stock
    in a Pittsburgh company called H. J. Heinz,
  and he felt it was his obligation,
    his obligation,
  to go over to the north side of town,
    to walk through the plant at least once a year
      and talk with the workers
    to be sure that they were treated right
      and that the product was a good one.
I am amazed by the fact that many who own stock today
  do not even know what product is made,
    let alone by whom and where.
The principle we live by is:
  "Where and how my property was acquired
    or what I do with it
      is nobody's business but my own."
And it doesn't matter
  whether that is a little
    or a lot.
How insidious,
  how tempting, to rely on what we have.
For we know what we have
  and we can hold onto it . . . we think,
    and feel secure in it . . . we think.

We depend on what we have:

money, stock, securities, land, possessions,
    all of which are outside ourselves.
And our possessions not only possess us,
    they are the very ground of our identity.
But what becomes of us
    if we lose what we have?
        For, indeed, whatever a person has
            can be lost.

One of the most telling parables of Jesus is found only in Luke's Gospel:

> There was a rich man whose fields produced a bumper crop.
>   "What do I do now," he asked himself, "since I don't have any place to store my crops? I know!" he said, "I'll tear down my barns and build larger ones so I can store all my grain and my goods. Then I'll say to myself, 'You have plenty put away for years to come. Take it easy, eat, drink, enjoy yourself.'"
>   But God said to him, "You fool! This very night your life will be demanded back from you. All this stuff you've collected—whose will it be now?"

What a tale!
    Amassing a superabundance of material possessions
        for the sake of la dolce vita
            becomes the height of folly
        in the light of the responsibility of life itself
            and the assessments of it that will take place
                once it is over.
It is to be the ultimate fool,
    providing for the "having" life
    and losing eternal life.
Or, to put it in contemporary language,
    to put it where we all live,
        in the realm of "identity":

If I am what I have,
and if what I have is lost,
who, then, am I?
Nobody but a
defeated, deflated, pathetic testimony
to the wrong way of living,
because I can lose what I have,
and, therefore, I am constantly worried
that I shall lose what I have.
I'm afraid of thieves,
of economic dangers,
of revolutions,
of sickness,
of death.
And I am afraid
of love,
of freedom,
of growing,
of change,
of the unknown.
Therefore, I become
defensive,
hard,
suspicious,
lonely,
driven—
driven by the need to have more in order to be better protected.
But—
If I am who I am
and not what I have,
no one can deprive me of my identity.
No one can threaten my security.
My center is within my self.

My capacity for being and for expressing my
   essential powers
      is part of my character structure
         and depends on me.
Furthermore, while "having" is based on something that is diminished by
use,
      "being" grows by practice.
It' s like that bush Moses saw in the desert,
   on flame, burning, but not being consumed.
That is the paradox of the biblical teaching here.
The powers of being,
   of reason,
      of love,
         of artistic and intellectual creation,
   grow through the process of being expressed and used.
What is spent is not lost,
   but, on the contrary,
      what is kept is lost.
That is where Jesus' statement comes in to haunt us:
   "Who saves his life loses it
      but who loses it for my sake finds it."
Ultimately all are known
   by how they live,
      what they do,
         not by what they have.
Jesus said bluntly:
   "By their fruits you shall know them."
      And that came from an old proverb: "Like root, like fruit."
Roots that lie deeply in the soil of the self,
   the depth of our being,
      bring forth good fruit.
It has been the observation of such good fruit
   that has persuaded me to be a Christian,

for I have seen that
a person may hoard life,
but, in so doing, that person loses all that makes
life valuable to others
and worth living for the self.
The way to serve others is to live for others.
The way to fulfill God's purpose for us,
the way to happiness,
is to spend life,
for only by doing so will we find life
here and hereafter.

Some of you may remember John Cameron Swazey picking a certain
watch off the propeller of a boat,
holding it up to the camera
to show the second hand still moving,
and saying,
"It takes a licking and keeps on ticking."
Well I thought of that recently
while preparing for the Wills Emphasis Sunday.
Actually I thought of that in connection with a
woman in the congregation I served in Louisville.
I never knew Mary Schachner.
She joined the church in 1884 and died before I was born.
But she set up a trust as part of the endowment funds of that congregation
"to benefit the poor children
in the elementary and high schools of Louisville."
When I was interim pastor,
I had the wonderful experience of meeting with a
bank officer and the superintendent of the schools
to hear what Mary Schachner
was doing for the children that year.

What I heard was Mary Schachner's heart
  still ticking after all those years.
For that year Mary Schachner
  clothed 425 boys and 383 girls,
    by purchasing 1,008 pairs of socks,
    2,190 items of underwear,
    393 pairs of jeans,
    489 pairs of shoes,
    187 blouses and skirts, 8 sweaters, and 61 coats.
In addition she provided twelve needy students with eyeglass
prescriptions—
  for to learn effectively students must be able to see clearly.
All in all more than thirty-five hundred public school students
  were helped by the far-sighted Mary Schachner.
We have a lot of potential Mary Schachners here at Westminster.
  Some may even consider endowing their pledge
    so that they can keep on giving—
      providing for others the love, care, and concern
      that they enjoyed through this congregation
      after they are gone.
It's part of Christian stewardship—
  and a way to "keep on ticking."
Mary Schachner is still known in Louisville today, long after her death.
She is known not by what she possessed
  but by what she gave away.
Central to this sermon today
  was one of the parables of Jesus.
    Jesus, the master storyteller,
      looked out and saw a farmer
        harvesting, storing,
      and turned it into a teaching.
How would Jesus end this sermon today?

What would he look out and see?
What story would he tell?
Let me try . . .
When Kay and I were working on our old house in Old Town
we came upon this lovely little
blue glass bottle in one of the walls.
Now this piece of blue glass
appears to be blue
when the light shines through it
because it absorbs all other colors
and, thus, does not let them pass.
That is to say,
we call the glass "blue"
precisely because it does not retain the blue waves.
It is named not for what it possesses
but for what it gives out.

So the text of the day really asks,
"By what name are you called?"

PART FOUR

ILLUSTRATIONS AND OTHER WORSHIP RESOURCES

1. A CALL TO WORSHIP

(ADAPTED FROM PSALM 104)

One: O God, from the sky you send rain on the hills
All: And the earth is filled with your blessings.
One: You make fresh grass grow for cattle,
All: And fruit for your people.
One: You bring forth food from the earth:
All: Wine to make us rejoice,
One: Oil to make us cheerful,
All: And bread to give us strength.
One: Let us sing praise to this God who gives us all good things.

2. STEWARDSHIP DEDICATION DAY PRAYER

O God, we have come before you this day in great anticipation—
We have walked up and presented ourselves anew to you—
   presented ourselves in forms both seen and unseen.
Throughout the ages you have asked nothing but love
   from your people.
We know that we must act out that love
   always giving our love first to you . . .

God of love—pluck the world out of our hearts
   loosen the chains of attachment.
Hurl the world into our hearts—
   where we can carry it with you
   in infinite tender care
   to share what we have.
Help us assume the discipline

to live in simplicity,
    avoiding greed and luxury
    that threaten our neighbor's survival.
So may our stewardship encompass our whole manner of living,
    the needs of others,
    the beauty, order, health, and peace
    of the entire universe.
So now we present our offerings
    of self—of money—of intentions—of love
    in the name of Jesus who has so shown us your love
    and taught us to pray: Our Father . . .

3. A DECLARATION OF FAITH

God made us to care for other created things.
    God made human beings along with all the other creatures
    and charged them to care for the earth
    and all that lives on it.

We acknowledge we share in the interdependence
    that binds together all God's creation.
Yet God gives us power to rule and tame,
    to order and reshape the world.
We hold the earth in trust
    for future generations of living things.
The Lord forbids us to plunder, foul, and destroy the earth.
The Lord expects us to produce, to consume, to reproduce
    in ways that make earth's goodness available to all people and reflect
    God's love for all creatures.
The Lord bids us use our technical skills
    for beauty, order, health, and peace.
        (From *A Declaration of Faith*, chapter 2, no. 3)

Christ teaches us
   to go beyond legal requirements
   in serving and helping our neighbor,
   to treat our neighbor's needs as our own,
   to care passionately for the other's good,
   to share what we have.
It is part of our discipline
   to live in simplicity,
   avoiding greed and luxury
   that threaten our neighbor's survival.
We are obligated to speak the truth in love,
   to listen with patience and openness,
   to love our enemies,
   to accept the risk and pain that love involves.
     (From *A Declaration of Faith*, chapter 9, no. 4)

4

In 1994 Americans spent considerably more
   on lotteries than they gave to their churches.
   That year they spent
   $26.6 billion on lotteries
   and gave only
   $19.6 billion to their churches.

5

Once there was a Christian,
   He had a pious look,
His consecration was complete
   Except his pocketbook.
He'd put a dollar in the plate
   And then with might and main

He'd sing,
   "When we asunder part,
   It gives me inward pain."

6

In the Dark Ages when Christianity was making its first impact on north-
ern Europe, large numbers of the savage tribe of Franks were immersed
by walking them through a river and calling them baptized—and therefore Christian. But they were not quite sure that they wanted to give up
their savage battle attitudes. So the story is told that many would go into
the water holding their battle axes out of the water and saying, "This hand
has never been baptized," so that they could swing it again in slaughter.

   Well we do not carry battle axes today—they are rather inconvenient—
but we do carry pocketbooks and wallets, and often Christian people seem
to lift high their wallets and by their meager contributions proclaim, "This
pocketbook has never been baptized!"

7. WITH APOLOGIES TO WILLIAM SHAKESPEARE . . .

To pledge or not to pledge—that is the question.
Whether 'tis nobler in a man
To take the gospel free and let another foot the bill,
Or sign a pledge and pay toward church expenses!
To give, to pay—aye, there's the rub. To pay,
When on the free pew plan, a man may have
A sitting free and take the gospel too,
As though he paid, and none be aught the wiser.

To err is human, and human too, to buy
At cheapest rate. I'll take the gospel so!
For others do the same—a common rule!
I'm wise. I'll wait, not work—I'll pray, not pay.

And let the other fellow foot the bills,
And so I'll get the gospel free, you see!

But there is no cheap grace—
    It cost God his son.

8

The minster was giving a sermon on "total giving." When it came time to take up the offering, the plate came to a pew where there was a very small boy. He looked up at the usher and said, "Could you lower the plate?" Thinking that he wanted to see into the plate, the usher held it down a bit. "No," said the boy, "a little lower please." The usher lowered it a bit more. "More; could you just put it on the floor?" the boy asked. The usher was aghast but finally put it on the floor. The boy stepped into it, stood there, and said, "This is what I give to the Lord."

9

Sam came into the pastor's office, his face slightly twisted with a look that wanted to portray wisdom but instead expressed pain. "Brother Jim," he said, "I've been doing so well in my business—been making so much money lately—that I can't afford to tithe anymore."

Brother Jim grabbed Sam by the shoulders and forced him down on his knees. Then he knelt beside him with his hand on his shoulder and prayed, "O Lord, lower this man's income so he can tithe again."

10

The problem with most of us
    is that our net income
        doesn't keep up
           with our gross habits.

11

At a church meeting a very wealthy man rose to tell the rest of those present about his Christian faith. "I am a millionaire," he said, "and I attribute it all to the rich blessings of God in my life. I remember that turning point in my faith. I had just earned my first dollar and I went to a church meeting that night. The speaker was a missionary who told about his work. I know that I only had that dollar bill in my pocket and had to either give it all to God's work or nothing at all. So at that moment I decided to give my whole dollar—everything I had—to God. I believe that God blessed that decision, and that is why I am a rich man today."

He finished and there was an awed silence at his testimony as he moved toward his seat. As he sat down, a little old lady sitting in the same pew leaned over to him and said, "I dare you to do it again."

12

There are three kinds of giving:
    grudge giving,
        duty giving,
            and thanksgiving.
Grudge giving says, "I have to,"
    duty giving says, "I ought to,"
        thanksgiving says, "I want to."
The first comes from constraint,
    the second from a sense of obligation,
        the third from a full heart.
Nothing much is conveyed in grudge giving since
    "The gift without the giver is bare."
Something more happens in duty giving,
    but there is no song in it.
Thanksgiving is an open gate into
    the love of God.

(R. N. Rodenmayer, *Thanks Be to God*)

The Eight Degrees of Charity

The First

and lowest degree is to give, but with reluctance or regret. This is the gift of the hand, but not of the heart.

The Second

is to give cheerfully, but not proportionately to the distress of the sufferer.

The Third

is to give cheerfully and proportionately but not until solicited.

The Fourth

is to give cheerfully, proportionately, and even unsolicited, but to put it in the poor man's hand, thereby exciting in him the painful emotion of shame.

The Fifth

is to give charity in such a way that the distressed may receive the bounty, and know their benefactor, without their being known to him . . .

The Sixth

which rises still higher, is to know the objects of our bounty but remain unknown to them . . .

The Seventh

is still more meritorious, namely, to bestow charity in such a way that the benefactor may not know the relieved persons, nor they the names of their benefactors . . .

The Eighth

and most meritorious of all, is to anticipate charity by preventing poverty; namely, to assist the reduced fellow-man, either by a considerable gift, or a sum of money, or by teaching him a trade, or by putting him in the way of business, so that he may earn an honest livelihood, and not be forced to the dreadful alternative of holding out his hand for charity. (Rabbi Moses Ben Maimonides, Spanish philosopher, A.D. 1135)

13. HISTORICAL STATEMENTS ON TITHING

By the grace of Christ (dearest brethren) the day is now at hand in which we ought to gather the harvest, and, therefore, should be thinking about returning thanks to God who gave it, both in the matter of making offerings and rendering tithes. For God who has deigned to give the whole has condescended to seek back from us the tithe, doubtless for our profit, not his own. (Augustine, A.D. 354–430)

What I spent I had,
    What I kept I lost,
    What I gave I have. (Henry Ward Beecher, 1813–1877)

14

This was in my file from 1958. . . . Ah, those were the days!

Three thousand for my convertible,
Five thousand for a piece of sod,
Ten thousand I paid to be in a house,
A dollar I gave to God.
A sum to entertain

My friends in endless chatter,
And when the world goes crazy mad,
I ask, "Lord, what's the matter?"
Yet there is one big question—
And for its answer I now search:
With things so bad in this old world,
What's holding back my church?

15. ANOTHER OLD ONE

Once there was a Christian,
He had a pious look—
His consecration was complete
Except his pocketbook.
He'd put a nickel in the plate,
And then with might and main
He'd sing, "When we asunder part
It gives me inward pain."
(Anonymous)

16

And when no one wants to try anything different for the annual campaign:

If you always do what you have always done,
You will always get what you always got.

If you always get what you have always got,
You will always think the way you always thought.

If you always think the way you always thought,
You will always act like you always acted.

If you always act the way you always acted,
Then you will always do what you have always done.

Oh why is it so hard for us to change—it's fun!
(Ruling Elder David Lee)

17

A translation from Dr. Moffatt:

> Amid a severe ordeal of trouble, their overflowing joy and their deep poverty together have poured out a flood of rich generosity; I can testify that up to their means, aye and beyond their means, they have given—begging me of their own accord, most urgently, for the favor of contributing to the support of the saints. They have done more than I expected: they gave themselves to the Lord to begin with. (2 Cor. 8:2–5)

18

. . . Preferring to store her money in the stomachs of the needy rather than to hide it in a purse. (Saint Jerome, in a letter to Principia, A.D. 400)

19

Will those of you who have been putting buttons in the collection basket, kindly put in your own buttons, and not those from the church upholstery. (Notice in a Scottish Presbyterian Church)

20. THE EXPLOSIVE SUBJECT OF TITHING

I don't know how many times people have come up to me and said that tithing is an "old Jewish custom" or "something out of the Old Testament" and therefore not for Christians. Well I don't recall anywhere that Jesus spoke against it and, after all, the Old Testament was the scripture of Jesus.

Then some who do think that it's a valid concept want to debate with me how to interpret the tithe—for example, before or after taxes?

I like to point such people to a neat passage in Leviticus that tells that when our mothers and fathers in the faith brought in their tithes, they did a good deal more.

> On the fifteenth day of the same month the festival of uncleaned bread in honor of the Eternal begins . . . for the seven days you must make a fire-offering to the Eternal . . . you shall bring a sheaf from the first-fruits of your harvest to the priest who shall wave the sheaf to and fro before the Eternal that you may be accepted. On the day you wave the sheaf, you must offer an unblemished yearling male-lamb as a burnt-offering to the Eternal; its cereal-offering shall be a fifth of a bushel of fine flour, mixed with oil, as an offering to be burned to the Eternal for a soothing odor, the libation of wine being three pints. Till you have brought the offering for your God, you must not eat, neither bread nor grain, roasted or fresh. This is a standing rule for all time and for all the country.
>
> From the day after the Sabbath, you shall count seven full weeks, and then you shall make a cereal-offering to the Eternal. You shall bring forward two loaves to be waved, made of a fifth of a bushel of fine flour, baked with dough, as first-fruits for the Eternal. With this bread you shall present seven unblemished yearling lambs, one young bullock, and two rams; they are to be a burnt-offering for the Eternal, with the usual cereal-offering and libation; also you shall offer a he-goat for a sin-offering, two yearling male-lambs as a recompense-offering; these the priest shall wave to and fro along with the bread of the first-fruits. This is a standing order for you and your descendants, for the whole country. When you reap your harvest you must not reap the field to the very corners, nor gather the stray ears of the harvest, but leave these for the poor folk and resident aliens: I am the Eternal your God. (Lev. 23:6–22.)

21

A vain man's motto is: Win gold and wear it.
A generous man's: Win gold and share it.
A miser's: Win gold and hoard it.
A prodigal's: Win gold and spend it.
A broker's: Win gold and lend it.
A gambler's: Win gold and lose it.
A Christian's: Win gold and use it.

(Anonymous)

22. MAMMON IS WISER THAN THE DICTATOR

What characterizes our society is the unique value ascribed to money. People in every age have coveted wealth, but few societies have lionized the entrepreneur as ours does. Aristocratic societies—and most societies have been aristocratic—have tended to look down on acquisitiveness and to despise merchants. Modern capitalism, by contrast, has made wealth the highest value. Our entire social system has become an "economy"; no earlier society would have characterized itself thus. Profit is the highest social good. Consumerism has become the only universally available mode of participation in modern society. The work ethic has been replaced by the consumption ethic, the cathedral by the sky scraper, the hero by the billionaire, the saint by the executive, religion by ideology. The Kingdom of Mammon exercises constraint by invisible chains that drives its slaves with invisible prods. (How rare it is for rich people to say, "I have enough.") But Mammon is wiser in its way than the dictator, for money enslaves not by force but by love. (Walter Wink, *Engaging the Powers: Discernment and Resistance in a World of Domination*, Minneapolis: Fortress Press, 1992, p. 54)

23. AN OLD ILLUSTRATION

A poor man who begged for food all his life found out that the king was coming to town. He decided to go out early, get a good place by the side of the road, meet him when he arrived, and ask the king for a gift. He found a perfect place for the confrontation, and began to wait. In his pouch the poor man had some fruit, a sandwich, a piece of meat, and a few coins. The day wore on, and no king.

Finally the king came down the road. The poor man got to his feet, shoved and got to a place close by where the king would come. He called out to the king, imploring him, "Good sir, I am one of your poor servants, take mercy upon me and give me a coin."

But the king looked down at him and said, "You give me a gift!"

The poor man was stunned! He cowered, groveled, but the demand of the king held. So he finally reached into his pouch and searched. First he pushed aside the sandwich and the fruit. Then he pushed aside the coins. Finally he found three crumbs in the bottom of the pouch. These he gave to the king.

The king went on his way, and the beggar went to his hovel and cried. That night, when he dumped out the contents of his pouch, he discovered that where the three crumbs had been there were now three gold pieces, shaped exactly to the size of the former crumbs.

"Why," he moaned, "did I not give the king my best?"

24. AN EMBARRASSMENT AT CUSTOMS

One of the most embarrassing things that happened to me on a trip Kay and I took to England a couple years ago happened when we came back through customs in New York.

Now we have traveled a good bit, some of it in the "gamier" parts of the world. We've been through all kinds of customs stations, and I have been asked time and again, "What have you to declare?" Mostly they take your word for it, but in the United States, they don't. Here they do search your baggage, especially if you tell them that in the box labeled on the outside in bold letters, "Kentucky Fried Chicken," you have a Victorian coal bucket.

So it was suitcase time for me, and then before the eyes of the waiting crowd the agent proceeds to hold up my dainties for inspection. And let me tell you, the most startling discovery was when this male found that his wife had stashed some of her dainties in *my* luggage!

Well I got to dreaming about that one night not long ago, and my dream went a little farther. I wondered how it would go when we come at the last great frontier, and the customs inspector of all customs inspectors asks that question, "What have you to declare?"

How embarrassing it will be for some who will stand at those gates and have to declare that they were dull-eyed travelers in this world, that all they can declare after their trip of life is $402,649 or, if they are from a lower income bracket, $10,264 and a secondhand car. As these poor slobs stand before the celestial customs officer with their battered suitcases of life, all they will be able to declare is a little tinsel from the five-and-dime of life.

But some will be able to say with Paul, " 'I declare the whole wide world' For I have allowed myself to be used in the service of the creator of the world. As I have traveled through the earth, I used the great percentage of my life to bring the words of life to others. So I declare this soul and that soul. This one fed, that one clothed. This one given a cup of cold water, this one visited in the prison of torment. This one picked up and loved . . . "

And the celestial customs inspector will say, "Well done, good and faithful traveler; enter into the Promised Land."

25

From a newspaper account:

> When the landing gear of US Airways Flight 479 collapsed last Friday at Charlotte and the crew ordered an evacuation down the emergency slides, almost half the passengers reacted by grabbing for their carry-on luggage. . . . One man grabbed two bags. Another struggled with a large bag. A woman blocked the aisle struggling to get a garment bag out of an overhead bin.

No comment needed.

26

In the comics I saw a cartoon, Pontius' Puddle. In this one the pastor is shown giving Pontius a basket full of fruit, saying, "Here Pontius. I'm giving food baskets to members who earn below the poverty line." Pontius asks, "What made you think my salary is that small?" The pastor's response: "I took your annual giving to the church and multiplied by ten!"

27. A PRAYER FOR MEALS

Jesus taught his disciples to pray, saying, "Give us this day our daily bread. . . . " And before each meal our mothers and fathers in the faith, in ancient times and still today, pray:

> Blessed art Thou,
> O Lord our God,
> King of the world,
> Who bringest forth bread from the earth.

28. THE MEANING OF GIVING

Kahlil Gibran—poet, philosopher, artist, born in Lebanon—gives us a wonderful passage on the meaning of giving in his book *The Prophet*.

> Then said a rich man, Speak to us of Giving.
>> And he answered:
>> You give but little when you give of your possessions.
>> It is when you give of yourself that you truly give.
>> Of what are your possessions but things you keep and guard for
>>> fear you may need them tomorrow?
> And tomorrow, what shall tomorrow bring to the over prudent dog burying bones in the trackless sand as he follows the pilgrims to the holy city?
>> And what is fear of need but need itself?

Is not dread of thirst when your well is full, the thirst that is
unquenchable?

There are those who give little of the much which they have—
    and they give it for recognition and their hidden desire makes
    their gifts unwholesome.
And there are those who have little and give it all.
These are the believers in life and the bounty of life, and their
    coffer is never empty.
There are those who give with joy, and that joy is their reward.
And there are those who give with pain, and that pain is their
    baptism.
And there are those who give and know not pain in giving, nor
    do they seek joy, nor give with mindfulness of virtue;
They give as in yonder valley the myrtle breathes its fragrance
    into space.
Through the hands of such as these God speaks, and from behind
    their eyes He smiles upon the earth.

It is well to give when asked, but it is better to give unasked,
    through understanding;
And to the open-handed the search for one who shall receive is
    joy greater than giving.
And is there aught you would withhold?
All you have shall some day be given;
Therefore give now, that the season of giving may be yours and
    not your inheritors'.

You often say, "I would give, but only to the deserving."
The trees in your orchard say not so, nor the flocks in your pasture.
They give that they may live, for to withhold is to perish.
Surely he who is worthy to receive his days and his nights, is
    worthy of all else from you.
And he who has deserved to drink from the ocean of life deserves
    to fill his cup from your little stream.

And what desert greater shall there be, than that which lies in the
  courage and the confidence, nay the charity, of receiving?
And who are you that men should rend their bosom and unveil
  their pride, that you may see their worth naked and their pride
  unabashed?
See first that you yourself deserve to be a giver, and an instrument
  of giving.
For in truth it is life that gives unto life—while you, who deem
  yourself a giver, are but a witness.
And you receivers—and you are all receivers—assume no weight
  of gratitude, lest you lay a yoke upon yourself and upon him
  who gives.
Rather rise together with the giver on his gifts as on wings;
For to be over mindful of your debt, is to doubt his generosity
  who has the free-hearted earth for mother, and God for father.
(Kahlil Gibran, *The Prophet*, New York: Alfred A. Knopf, 1980, pp. 19–22)

29.

Some have too much, yet still do crave;
  I little have, and seek no more.
They are but poor, though much they have,
  And I am rich with little store.
They poor, I rich; they beg, I give;
  They lack, I leave; they pine, I live.
                    (Sir Edward Dyer, ?–1607)

30. A PRAYER ON COMMITMENT SUNDAY

O Lord of us all, you who call us to be stewards of this earth—
We hold in these baskets our commitments to you.
It is more than pieces of paper saying what we intend to give;
    it is our covenant-keeping,
    it is our discipleship,
    it is our prayer that we gather in these baskets.

We give you this morning not only our commitments
  but we give to you the promise of
      our time, our prayers, our hours of concern,
      our special talents, our creativity, our hard work,
      and our money.
We give it all to you now:
  our commitment alive and wondrous and full of hope.
We give it all in a spirit of cheerfulness and joy—
  give it to you who have gifted us
  with the bounty of your amazing grace.
In the name of one who gave his all—
  Jesus our Lord. Amen.

31. A MODERN PARABLE

Now it came to pass on a day at noon that I was the guest of a certain man. The lunch was enjoyed at a popular restaurant, and the waiters were very efficient, the food very good. Now when the end of the meal was at hand, the waiter brought unto my host the check. And my host examined it, frowned a bit, but made no comment. But as we arose to depart, I observed that he laid some bills under the edge of the plate, however I know not how many, but the waiter, who stood nearby, smiled happily, which being interpreted means that the tip was satisfactory.

Now with such customs we are all familiar and this parable entereth not into the merits or demerits of tipping. But as I meditated upon the coins and bills that become tips throughout our nation, I began to think of tips and tithes. For the proverbial tip should be at least a tithe lest the waiter turn against you, and now in our time it is proper to leave a tithe and a half!

As I continued to think on these things it came unto me that few people who go to church treat their God as well as they honor their waiter. For they give unto the waiter a tithe but unto God they give whatsoever they think will get them by.

Verily, doth man fear the waiter more than he feareth God, and doth he love God less than he loveth the waiter?

32. A STEWARDSHIP HYMN

God in His Love for Us Lent Us This Planet[1]

God in his love for us lent us this planet,
gave it a purpose in time and in space;
small as a spark from the fires of creation,
cradle of life and the home of our race.

Thanks be to God for its bounty and beauty,
life that sustains us in body and mind:
plenty for all, if we learn how to share it,
riches undreamed of to fathom and find.

Long have our human wars ruined its harvest:
long has Earth bowed to the terror of force;
long have we wasted what others have need of,
poisoned the fountain of life at its source.

Earth is the Lord's! It is ours to enjoy it,
ours as God's stewards, to farm and defend.
From its pollution, misuse and destruction,
good Lord, deliver us, world without end!

33. AND FINALLY . . .

Remember, what you render unto God is deductible from what you render unto Caesar.

---

[1]Text by Fred Pratt Green. © 1973 The Hymn Society. Administered by Hope Publishing Co., Carol Stream, IL 60188. All rights reserved. Used by permission.